BILLY GRAHAM
AND SEVEN WHO WERE SAVED

BILLY GRAHAM
and Seven Who Were Saved

LEWIS W. GILLENSON

Trident Press *New York, New York*   1967

This book, BILLY GRAHAM AND SEVEN WHO WERE SAVED, originated from a recently published article by Mr. Gillenson for *Good Housekeeping* Magazine.

LIBRARY OF CONGRESS CATALOG CARD NUMBER: 67–13570

PUBLISHED SIMULTANEOUSLY IN THE
UNITED STATES AND CANADA BY TRIDENT PRESS,
A DIVISION OF SIMON & SCHUSTER, INC.,
630 FIFTH AVENUE, NEW YORK, N.Y. 10020.

PRINTED IN THE UNITED STATES OF AMERICA

To Bernice, the perfect wife for an author
writing about faith

CONTENTS

BILLY GRAHAM

The Man and His Ministry

THE TWENTY-ODD years since the end of World War II has seen United States Christianity through some of its most turbulent phases. The desperateness of the war had encouraged reliance on a Super-being since it was patently obvious that the human species seemed to have offered nothing less than genocide and a counter-reaction to it that bred more "necessary" mass murder. In resignation, it became logical to hope, or insist, that the foxhole offered a cold haven for an atheist.

This emergency-inspired, God-centered outlook took a severe hiding with the advent of Hiroshima; one of the scientist creators of the Bomb viewed the fiery mushroom and dolefully observed that he had witnessed the fires of hell unleashed on man's kingdom. Whether out of fear or otherwise, the nation moved into a swift awareness of religious values. Church rolls grew; Christianity actually became popular and scholars talked tentatively about the "religious revival of the fifties."

Today those same scholars and churchmen are debating a new dialogue centered within the astonishingly titled "God Is Dead" thesis. Astonishing because its participants are men hardly indifferent to or enemies of religion, since most are Christian theologians intent upon articulating the spiritual temper of the times and finding doctrinal accommodation for it. The times are anti-metaphysical, they say. Faith is no longer a possession; it has been shriveled to a hope. Few really believe with immovable certitude that God, from a perch in heaven, made man in His image. And so they sadly deduce that since modern man doesn't feel God, commune with God, and take pragmatic guidance from Him, God for him is dead.

In a strongly prophetic way, Billy Graham, the uncomplicated farmer's son turned evangelist, anticipated this melancholy state of spiritual affairs. From the beginnings of his ministry following the war, he has continually warned that "cold" faith resting upon intellectuality is scholarship, not religion. He has proclaimed, sometimes at the cost of community comfort, that good social works alone are not synonymous with religion. In short, Graham refused to question the literal Word of God and thereby, to him, denigrate it. The Bible meant exactly what it said. And to know God, one could not sit calmly in a pew waiting for divine lightning to strike. Nor could one intellectualize oneself into faith. The process involved a giving of one's inner self, a bending of the will, a total surrender, an immersion of the ego before the superego of the universe. And with that condition, God reveals Himself as a living and enriching Being. The miracle of Jesus is its constant proof.

Today, after twenty-five years of preaching, Graham holds to his earliest thesis without a tremor of doubt. The seven persons described in this book represent sample witnesses among the hundreds of thousands who have come forward at his rallies all around the world to make their "decisions for Christ." They represent a fair cross section of our Christian community, engaged as they are in the professions, business, the arts, sports, politics and social life. Each suffered cruel need and each one found his answer simply and directly—a lance of love from God to the believer, without an earthly intercessor. All Graham did was to employ his uncanny pulpiteering talents in the persuasion that it could happen.

This intense man, not yet fifty, was catapulted to fame initially through his association with a professional hoodlum and a professional hillbilly. It all began in 1949 in Los Angeles, in a large circus tent, where he fulminated nightly against sin to tepid crowds that found him sincere, if not earthshaking. Then Stuart Hamblen, a gaudy cowboy crooner, announced to his fans that he had come crying at three in the morning to Graham, who had helped him surrender to his Savior. Hamblen forthwith abandoned the world of the bar and racetrack for the purer extracurricular environs of the Church. This he proudly proclaimed on his radio show. West Coast newspapers ran headlines about it. Attendance at Graham's meetings soared.

About the same time a fat little mobster named Mickey Cohen, who couldn't stay out of the headlines—and consequently out of trouble—mainly because he couldn't keep his mouth shut, decided to get into the act. He visited the tent and told everybody who would listen that he was "mighty interested in the possibilities of gettin' meself saved by this fella." Graham, who takes literally all that is in the Bible, especially those New Testament passages enjoining all Christians to go out and save the sinner, took on the challenge. Many of their meetings took place at odd hours. Much palaver was exchanged on the telephone. Mickey would wail, "The mob got Bugsy Siegel and they're out to get me. Preacher, what should I do?" Graham's urgings were simple and direct: Confess your sins and come to Christ. Graham kept the negotiations confidential until he read accurate verbatim reports about them supplied to the newspapers by the exhibitionistic hoodlum.

The publicity did little for the mobster's miseries. Long before he agreed to hand himself over to the Savior, the Feds took him in hand and a judge then delivered him to a penitentiary, where presumably he will have more time than it usually takes a Billy Graham sinner to make up his mind about repenting.

The publicity did, however, make Billy Graham famous. The crowds that came to hear him in Los Angeles started spilling over hours before the scheduled starting time of the meeting. Many other Hollywood "names" came and came forward. The curious came to look over the long, lean, youthful preacher with the hot blue eyes in the handsome, ascetic face, who spoke with the intensity of one who really believed that little time remained before the bludgeoning advent of final reckoning.

Despite his dramatic successes with Hollywood's worldly folk, Graham did not endear himself to all members of the clergy in the "sinful" City of Angels. Graham has, until a dozen years ago, appealed to a parochial minority in the Protestant fellowship. His evangelism at times seems anachronistic. He is a protagonist of what is commonly tagged "that old-time religion"—but with latter-day refinements. His religion itself is the simple, full-gospel message with the insistent proclamation that all men must repent in advance of the swiftly oncoming Judgment Day, or burn in hell. He preaches in the style and tradition of the old Methodist circuit rider of the frontier, whose saddlebags were crammed with Biblical tracts and whose heart so flowed with a love of God that it elevated him to flights of passionate oratory. His message sprang direct, unrefined, from the Bible. The cornerstone of mass Protestantism in this nation was formed by men like John Wesley and George Whitefield, who toured our outposts in the mid-eighteenth century, preaching simple words to simple people with overwhelming conviction.

The tradition was carried on by such acrobatic pulpiteers as Dwight Moody in the late nineteenth century and by Billy Sunday in the early twentieth century. Sunday, an ex-big-league ball player and convert from the demon rum, behaved on the lecture platform the way Willie Mays behaves in Candlestick Park. He punched the Bible, spun in somersaults, and hurtled his wiry body into space at an imaginary devil, all in the attempt to press home the point that you've got to keep punching at the devil before he delivers the payoff blow against you.

These homiletic calisthenics drew big audiences for Sunday. His listeners did not attend his meetings entirely out of theological conviction. Nobody could deny it; Sunday put on a darn good show.

But the organized churches of the land would have little part of him. Though he preached a nondenominational message,

Sunday hardly fitted into their concept of reflective Christians led by a trained ministry. Through the twenties, an era Graham thinks of with sadness as our age of disbelief, the likes of Sunday were as welcome in our organized churches as a guitar-picking rock-and-roller in a Bach chorale. But the summer sawdust trail, where traveling evangelists light fires under the faithless, never grew weeds. It is well stamped, especially in the rural South. It is from this tradition and from this area that William Franklin Graham and his theology spring.

Whether it is held in a tent or in a great hall of a big city, a Graham meeting keeps its atmosphere of camp-meeting excitement. Graham's teammates are accomplished in producing it and in stimulating their hundreds of volunteer workers to project it. In the early evening, the choir, which can range from a hundred to six thousand voices, drawn from all the sponsoring churches in the community, sings a few hymns. The chairman of the meeting then says a few words of greeting. An invocation is read, and Cliff Barrows comes forward. Barrows, a black-haired, handsome man in his middle forties, is a great favorite with Graham audiences. Holding his trombone high, he waves his arms in greeting, urging everybody to "meet the Christian brother or sister next to you. Shake his hand, c'mon, shake it again a good one, now introduce yourselves. Now, don't you wonderful folks just feel wonderful?" Sometimes he rehearses them in responses. "Say a big hallelujah, good and hard now, a big one," he pleads smilingly.

"Hallelujah!" the crowd roars.

"That's just grand. Now let's sing a few verses of 'Send a Great Revival to My Soul,' our team theme song."

Barrows leads the singing for a few minutes, waving like a football cheerleader. Then he draws his shiny trombone to his mouth and joins in. After a few hymns, he introduces George Beverly Shea. "Folks, here's Bev Shea, America's beloved gospel singer." Shea, a large, rawboned, Lincolnesque figure, has a deep, beautifully trained bass voice. The listeners become very still as he sings. They do not applaud when he finishes. The chairman of the meeting then makes a short plea for financial aid. In a remarkably short time, the dozens of ushers finish passing the collection plate. By this time Graham has come to the platform.

He pauses for an instant, looking over the great audience. In a businesslike manner he opens his soft leather-covered Bible, and in a strong, well-modulated baritone voice with a Southern flavor, he reads a passage setting forth his theme of the evening. He seems unaware of the lapel microphone he wears, so loudly does he speak. His body weaves in rhythm to his words; his fingers, like tendrils, climb above his head, tremble, stiffen and soften and move about as if they were turning a pair of huge dials in the air. He stares directly at his audience. His voice drops lower and lower, almost to a whisper. He hangs over the lectern and cocks his head sideways at the audience, absentmindedly sweeping a lock of hair from his forehead, which by this time is beaded with sweat. His eyes narrow; he cajoles and mimics, then suddenly stamps his foot, slams the Bible, spins halfway around, clenches his fist, and again throws his arms skyward.

"You and I deserve hell. You and I deserve to spend eternity separated from God. You and I have sinned. Oh, yes, the Scripture teaches that you're a sinner. And so am I. The Bible says I was born in sin. The Bible says that in sin did my mother conceive me. At this moment there is only a thread between you and eternity. Don't ever forget God is a god of love. God is Love. Yes, God is Love. I don't care whether it's adultery or filthiness or pride or murder or stealing or wine. Tonight God loves you! God wants you to know His son, Jesus Christ."

His voice again has dropped. He falls into a confidential manner, then moves into one of the older, surefire passages in his repertoire—the Daniel and the Lion parable.

"Old Dan," he says, "was the prime minister of one of the most powerful countries in the world and a pal of the boss—the King of the Medes and the Persians. Some jealous guys were out to get him, so they trained their spyglasses on him one morning when he was praying and had his Venetian blinds up. They tattled to the King. The King was in a spot, so he said to his lawyers, 'Find me a couple of loopholes so I can spring my pal Dan.'

Smart as those lawyers were, you know, they just couldn't find a loophole, and the King just had to send Dan to the lions. So what happens, old Daniel walks in. He's not afraid. He looks the first big cat in the eye, kicks him in the belly, and says, 'Move over, Leo, I want me a nice fat soft lion I can use for a pillow. I'm tired.' "

Graham drops the colloquialism and the cozy manner quickly. Once his point is made, he heads straight into his thesis again. The short homey insert is a psychological softening-up device to suspend the crescendo momentarily. Then, about twenty-eight minutes after he has begun, he throws the challenge at his audience.

"A lady came here the other night. She was not sure; she was not convinced. She did not come forward. She was still thinking about accepting Jesus as her Savior when she was struck with a heart attack and the life passed out of her body. And so far as I know, she was not reborn and she must pay the penalty forever— *forever!* Tonight you have a chance. Why don't you do business with God tonight? He wants you. He loves you. He's patient and He is waiting for you. Come to God tonight in true faith and you live *forever.* God will not spare you unless you stand clothed in the righteousness of Jesus Christ. You say, 'Well, Billy, what do I have to do?' All you have to do is let Jesus in. You say, 'Is it as simple as that?' It's as simple as ABC. It's as simple as falling off a log. You say, 'How long does it take?' Only a second, a twinkling of an eye. Right now where you sit, you can settle it and say yes to Christ for eternity, and I guarantee on the authority of God's word that you can know before you leave here tonight that you're going to heaven. Utterly sure. You can be certain that you'll escape the judgment of Almighty God. Shall we pray?"

During the entire sermon not one "amen," "hallelujah" or any other sound of exultation emanates from the crowd. Graham, in sublime control of his audience, never permits it to besmirch what he considers the holy dignity of the message. Once when he was haranguing the citizens of Los Angeles about the sinfulness of the town, a man in the congregation brayed a piercing "Hallelujah!" Graham spun in his direction and snapped, "Brother, that's nothing to shout hallelujah about. That's something you ought to be ashamed of."

Nor does he permit demonstrations of physical exultation or of flash healings. In the midst of a New England meeting a woman broke out with the news that the evangelist had healed her illness. Graham, who becomes distraught at such testimonials, sternly made the point that *he* healed no one. He had no such power, he said, and if a healing did in truth occur, it was God's alone, and in no way Billy Graham's.

After the prayer at the termination of Graham's sermon, he asks everyone to keep his head bowed. Then, as the choir sings the strains of the hymn "Just as I Am," he asks those that wish to come forward to raise their hands. A few hands rise. Some of the people are crying openly. He recognizes them, then more, all the time urging others to make their decisions and raise their hands. Finally he asks them to come forward to the platform before him. As they march down the aisles, the ushers representing all the participating church bodies come forward to intercept them. Graham, though a Baptist himself, has made no denominational appeal. The converts choose their own denominations. By the time they reach the platform, Graham has slipped away. At that point, associate evangelist Grady Wilson and the counselors take over, instructing the new converts on their future behavior in their respective churches.

The overall impact of Graham's sermons is a great deal less emotional or dramatic than it seems in the telling. He has no gift for the little story that brings laughs. He is confident that the audience does not need preparation for his personality; the people have come, he believes, because there is a great hunger at this time for God's message, and he, Graham, is just a handy instrument. The only so-called warm-up preparation is embodied in the spirit of the audience and of the music—all religious in tone. Throughout the two and a half hours of a typical meeting, Graham and his team allow no diversionary high jinks to water down that spirit. If a Graham meeting is a show, as some of his gradually diminishing list of detractors imply, Graham would say that God and Jesus Christ are the leading players, and the Bible is the script. Graham thinks of his own role as being not unlike that of a moderator on the side, who helps introduce these divine dramatis personae to the audience.

Nevertheless, Graham's modesty cannot hush the fact that no other personality in American history has ever realized such success in promoting that drama. In the late forties he was an unknown country preacher. By the spring of 1966, when he was preparing for his latest crusade into London, he had already preached to some tens of millions face to face in the largest cities in the world. Well over a million had come forward to declare themselves for Christ at his meetings. Millions more wrote letters testifying to their decisions after hearing Billy on his radio and television programs, "Hour of Decision." At one meeting in the Dallas Cotton Bowl, a cynic growled that the preacher's hypnotic eyes were drawing the audience. A team member answered gently, "Did you ever try looking into a man's hypnotic eyes when he's on the fifty-yard line and you are twenty yards behind the goal post?"

No such reasoning could have assuaged the snarling anger the British press had whipped up against Graham before he landed on British soil for his first London crusade in 1954. Once Graham had accepted the invitation of a joint ministerial association in London to conduct a revival campaign in England, his own emotions were whipped to a feverish desire to make the campaign a success. Wherever he traveled he begged people to pray for the success of the campaign and for "cold, near-atheistic England." At one point, five hundred different prayer groups all over the world were praying for "pagan England."

Long before he arrived in England, he had reason to know that if the British were cold or indifferent, it was not manifest in the pens of their press representatives. Those gentlemen slashed at him with their wit and they used the custard-pie-in-the-puss technique on him with deleterious effect.

The man they called in America "The Thunderer of Revival," "Gabriel in Gabardine," "Barrymore of the Bible," "God's Ball of Fire," and a dozen similar sobriquets was coming to save them from themselves. The British press ripped him apart in editorials. Two members of the British Labour Party politely stood up in the House of Commons and suggested, for the sake of peace, that Billy stay the devil out of their country. Cartoonists had a field day at his expense; one pictured him as a sort of Roy Rogers, with sombrero, chaps, and six-shooters, blasting out the gospel from atop a white cow pony. The fact that Graham planned to (and actually did) use Roy Rogers, his horse, Trigger, and Rogers' wife, Dale Evans, to help in the young people's services served only to lend validity to the picture.

Before he sailed into Southampton, Billy and his team of six were reading wireless reports of what they were in for. Every day they would all kneel and pray for the success of the mission. They promised each other that their personal deportment would be of the highest Christian type, so as to set a proper example. They vowed to answer the bitterest criticism with their work and good deeds. They transmitted this avowal to the twenty-five others, already in England, who would join the special Greater London Evangelistic Crusade team. The brickbats started flying before he embarked.

"Cassandra," the waspish columnist of London's *Daily Mirror,* was among the first to take aim. He sneered:

The man who said Britain is "almost pagan and a hairline from communism . . ." is the slickest opponent of iniquity I have ever met. John the Baptist would have been horrified at the beautifully cut dark, double-breasted jacket and the natty gray sponge bag pants. He's bursting at the mental seams with good will. "May the Lord Bless you real good," he says. . . . He has a ferocious cordiality that scares ordinary sinners stone cold. . . . As soon as he switches on his luminous bulging goodness of heart . . . I reckon he ought to make us cockneys feel damned well ashamed of ourselves.

When Graham read the column, he said to Cliff Barrows, "Now, here's a fellow knows how to use the English language."

He wrote Cassandra a fan letter, asking to meet the author.

Cassandra agreed, on one condition: that the evangelist "meet this sinner on sinners' ground." They met at a popular pub called, whimsically enough, The Baptist's Head, located on St. John's Lane.

While Cassandra quaffed his ale, Graham sipped lemonade. He refrains from smoking, drinking and dancing simply because of habits instilled in him as a boy in North Carolina.

"I remember back home on the farm my dad whacked the daylights out of me for chewing a bit of tobacco," Graham says. "He fired the hired man who gave me the stuff, even though he had worked for us a long time and was a family friend. I used to think Dad did it for religious reasons, but I doubt it now. Dad used to chew tobacco himself, and I don't think the Bible made him stop."

At the St. John's Lane pub that day with Cassandra, Graham just sipped his lemonade.

Cassandra must have been impressed with the fresh candor of the young preacher. In a subsequent column he wrote, "I think he is a good man and simple. Goodness and simplicity are two tough customers. I never thought that simplicity could cudgel us so hard. We live and we learn."

The first meeting at Harringay Arena, a London sports palace normally a showcase for wrestlers, fighters, bike riders, and trapeze artists, was packed with twelve thousand curious souls. The meeting captivated London; not, as might be expected, because of the American's throbbing showmanship, but because the mood of the meeting was precisely the opposite of what the audience had expected. One writer said later, "Except for that vast choir—eleven hundred voices—going full out on their top notes, there was nothing to jerk a tear from the most hydromanic eye."

Another wrote:

He is not a particularly good preacher. But it doesn't matter. This is the ultimate spiritual energy that has always changed the world . . . that sent ragged crusades from the depths of Europe to Jerusalem . . . that sent the armies of Islam to storm the gates of Vienna and scale the Pyrenees. . . . And to release this energy it has taken a tall

young American with a good profile, a choir leader and a solo singer
with a pleasant voice . . . here were hundreds of people who had
made . . . the "Leap in the Dark." And a choir was singing, with
complete fervor, impossible things . . . an eternal life . . . paradise.
. . . And ten thousand more voices joined in. Here were . . . people
who had forgotten about the pay claim . . . the desire for a refrigera-
tor and a car . . . who had forgotten the whole materialistic philos-
ophy. "This is the way . . . the truth" and it made nonsense of most
of the speeches of most of the statesmen of the world.

The wondering enthusiasm of the writer reflected the British attitude toward Graham's mission. For three months they packed the arena. Once he visited at small Cliff College in a Methodist town on the outskirts of London. On a dreary wet morning more than sixty thousand people made the pilgrimage to stand on the campus grass and hear Graham. By midafternoon the campus had emptied out. That evening the narrow roads of the hamlet again groaned under the traffic of cars, bicycles, motorcycles and buses.

"Sixty thousand more came again," said Graham, talking like a man who had seen a miracle and couldn't quite believe he was still alive to talk about it. "It was still pouring and miserably cold. And when we left them later in the evening, they stayed on in the rain singing praises to God in one great swell. Lord, it was a sight I'll never forget. It had nothing to do with me. When I stood on the campus and talked I could feel the presence of God right next to me giving me a lift. These people wanted God's word desperately. The country was starved for God."

The crusade roared on to its final day, Saturday, May 22, when in two meetings more than 185,000 people packed the Wembley Stadium. A six-thousand-voice choir sang with heavenly fervor as four thousand people walked down the aisle to salvation.

At the end Graham stood shaking his head. "I was sure our efforts would fail in this country," he said. "And yet we did say again and again, if we did, the failure would be ours, not God's. Just look, the Lord's been mighty good."

In the twelve weeks of his crusade Graham spoke to more

than two million people. Almost forty thousand registered their decisions for Christ in answer to his entreaties. The Archbishop of Canterbury, the leader of the conservative Church of England, who was thought of as the spiritual opponent of Graham's expressive evangelism, sat on the platform at the last session, thus placing the Church's official stamp of approval upon his efforts. "I regard the campaign conducted by Dr. Graham as . . . a very humble, sincere and fruitful work of evangelism," he said. "I have noted with approval, first, the way in which Dr. Graham has avoided all unwise exploitation of the emotions, and secondly, his deliberate policy of sending people touched by him on to the regular Christian life and fellowship of their churches."

Graham had come prepared with thirty sermons and had to compose thirty more. Wherever he walked, crowds trailed after him. On the outside of the small hotel where he lived, an autograph-seeking crowd kept constant vigil. When Mrs. William Franklin Graham, Sr., Billy's mother, flew to London to be with her son for a few days, she was treated like royalty.

"Why, you just wouldn't have dreamed it, you know," she said. "They were following Billy around as if he were a celebrity or a movie star."

The adulation troubled Graham deeply. He read his Bible and was warned by its injunction to beware when all men speak too kindly of one.

So complete had been the turnabout in opinion that certain writers were taking it upon themselves to urge the local clergy to borrow a few tactics from Graham's book. Said one: "If Billy can rekindle the faith that makes life worth living, then would it be wrong to doubt the sincerity of his mission just because he surrounds it with the trappings of modern propaganda? Why should we assume that it is only the Devil that can get himself organized?"

One editorial churlishly said:

Our churches are dim, dull and musty as morgues. Instead of dressing the rest of us, our churchmen wear outdated ecclesiastical uni-

forms. Even modern parsons who find their dog collars irksome feel they have to knuckle under to dead tradition. Why? Who made the greatest impact on Wembley, bareheaded Billy with his informal dress or the Archbishop in his gaiters? . . . Our churchmen affect a dreary sexless drone in their services. . . . At every Billy Graham meeting you could hear people laughing. . . . Why, like the walls of Jericho, the church—or at least the parson—might come atumbling down.

At the end of the London crusade, Graham took off for two weeks of preaching on the Continent. He spoke in Denmark, Holland, Germany, France, Finland and Sweden. Graham, who speaks no foreign language, spoke through interpreters; when he would finish one fiery passage, the interpreter would translate, imitating his tone of voice and his gestures.

As he preached in a public hall in Paris, the food concessionaire sent his vendors, girls with tight black skirts slit high up the thigh, down the aisles to hawk their wares. Somehow they failed to tarnish the glow of the meeting. Graham thought of it as just one more of those strange things you encounter in Paris.

The Communists hopped on him for his efforts, charging that the small cards (actually announcements of conversion) that Graham's ushers collected were to become the nucleus of an American file of espionage agents. Graham viewed that as flattery of Christianity. "If they are that frightened of a good Christian," he says, "I'm glad to know it."

His tour through Europe gave him a little time to mull over the hectic events in England, and gave the British an opportunity to sort out their thoughts about him. Even at their most enthusiastic, the British never really figured out the inner compulsions of such as Billy Graham. To a nation that reveres understatement and calm in all affairs from politics to war and religion, Graham never quite stopped being an enigma. A welcome one, perhaps, but still an enigma.

One writer, William Hickey, the sharp-penned columnist of Lord Beaverbrook's *Daily Express,* said that it never made him anything but embarrassed to talk with Graham about crusades, evangelism and the Holy Spirit right after breakfast. He paid tribute to Graham's modesty in saying, when he was compared to the great religious leader John Wesley, "I'm not fit to carry his shoelaces." He was struck by Graham's sincere convictions in favor of abolishing denominational differences in Protestantism and effecting unity among all the church groups. He reported how Graham recoiled at the idea that perhaps he would found a new church. "I have absolutely not one new idea to contribute to a new church. The idea is opposed to everything I believe."

When people are bewildered by his demonstrative religious passion, Graham is in turn bewildered that they can be indifferent about God. All his life he has carried God on his sleeve with the naturalness of a football hero wearing a varsity letter on his chest. What he brought to religion was no novelty of interpretation, no special pulpiteering gimmick. By his own admission, he is not a particularly original preacher. His homely sign-off on his radio-TV broadcasts, "May God bless you real good," is an indication of his effective informality as well as an exceptionally memorable tag line.

Were Graham to fit the stereotype of the God-fearing full-gospel preacher, his manner should be that of the stern, angry, self-righteous man of God with flaring nostrils, flaming eyes and an authoritative finger pointing in the direction of hell or heaven with an accuracy of which only people boasting of built-in pipe-lines to God can feel certain. Actually, Graham is more the small-town Rotarian, in the most favorable sense of the term. He functions professionally—even in the presence of what others might consider abject sinfulness—with optimism and a happy absence of self-righteousness. Whatever prejudices he was fed in his provincial youth have been watered down with the passage of time. Contact with the thousands of people of contrasting personalities and outlook to whose points of view he has eagerly exposed himself through the years—all of whom find him an absorbing listener—have helped considerably.

Once he was sitting in a Southern restaurant with a Jewish

friend with whom he enjoys exploring religious and political philosophy. As their discussion grew heated, an elderly lady approached their table. Looking directly into the eyes of Graham's friend and holding out her hand, she said, "Why, Billy Graham, this is a wonderful moment. Imagine seeing you here! We prayed for you over there."

His friend gently corrected her, pointing to the real Billy Graham, on the opposite side of the table. Hesitating not at all, the lady poured out her enthusiasm, requesting that Graham come to another part of the restaurant, where she would like him to greet a dozen young ladies from her church who were attending a local religious convention. Graham graciously moved with her to the back of the restaurant, while his friend moved to the front and waited for him there. A moment later the same lady walked up to the front of the restaurant and asked Graham's friend:

"Are you a Baptist, young man?"

"No, ma'am, I'm not."

"A Methodist?"

"No."

"Well, are you—er—" she began.

Graham's friend said quietly, "Ma'am, I'm an orthodox Jew."

The lady blanched. She searched his face carefully. "Is Reverend Graham converting you?" she asked sharply.

"No, ma'am, he's not," he answered with twinkling eyes. "Seems to me that I might be having more success in getting him over to our side."

The lady looked at him aghast. "You know, young man," she said accusingly, "I thought you looked Jewish when I saw you." Then she flounced to the back of the room.

Later, as Graham walked with his friend down the street, he listened to the story in amazement.

"First the good lady welcomes you as Billy Graham and then she says you looked Jewish all the time. Partner," he said, placing an arm on his friend's shoulder in apology, "there's all sorts of folks. Some are tolerant and some are—well, you know. . . ."

On the platform Graham allows himself little luxury of interpretation or tortuous reappraisal of the Biblical message. There is absolutely no doubt in his mind as he says, slapping the Bible he usually carries with him (he beats eight a year into pulp), "All the world's answers are right in this little book."

One clergyman, a Princeton intellectual, summed it up this way:

"I wouldn't know how to preach like Graham. For twenty years now I have been engaged, like most of our so-called modern preachers, in inventing logic, parable, intellectual forensics and everything but the words of the Bible to prove that they are not wrong. Here comes this fellow who says the Bible is right because he believes in God; the Scriptures are God's words. That's simply it. No need to fiddle around with any more proof than that. Furthermore, I'd hate to admit it, but I think most of us were rather insecure about our congregations; we were afraid that they would think we were old fuddy-duddies if we just opened the Bible and read from it and told a few of its stories with complete belief. What Graham has done is to give those old words new dignity. And, brother, how we need it in these times!"

In discussing the Scriptures, Graham not only accepts the idea of a literal heaven and hell and a real devil, but brushes away any modernistic twaddle concerning their possible symbolic nature.

People used to laugh at the devil, he claims, because they were afraid of him. "They pictured him as a grotesque, foolish creature with horns and a long tail. They put a pitchfork in his hands and a feebleminded leer on his face. . . . Actually he is a creature of vastly superior intelligence. His reasoning is brilliant, his plans ingenious, his logic almost irrefutable. He is no bungling creature. He is a prince of lofty stature, of unlimited craft and cunning, able to turn every situation to his own advantage."

Graham explains his ministry in terms of God's command

—or will. Belief, he says, is a two-way street: "You pray and you tell God that you believe. You trust in Him. You present Him with a problem, and if you have real faith, you get an answer. No question about it. I'm a preacher because God ordained I should be one. That's it."

It would almost seem that anyone professing such a direct affiliation with his God should look or sound or act like a mystic. When Graham expresses these convictions, he's about as mystical as a college coach whipping up the boys at half time. His eyes shine with spirit. He looks directly at you, almost defiantly, as if to ask how in thunder you can believe anything but this.

Graham's parents, who were solid, God-fearing farm folks, reared Billy, their oldest child, in this religious atmosphere. The dairy farm the Grahams called home was settled soon after the Civil War by the elder Graham's grandfather. It consisted of 275 acres eminently suitable for dairy farming, a few miles outside Charlotte, North Carolina, in rolling mountain country. Get off the main highway, walk into a thicket near the Graham brook, let your imagination roam, and you can picture this as pre-Civil War country, unchanged since those colorful days. The countryside is conservative; the people are deeply rooted in their homes, their traditions and their faith.

For a generation Charlotte and its environs have been a hospitable way stop for streams of revivalists who regularly have fired the faith of the populace. Morrow Coffee Graham, Billy Graham's mother, was born a few miles from the Graham farm. Both she and William Franklin Graham were members of the Associate Reformed Presbyterian Church. They married after a five-year courtship and moved into a log cabin on the farm grounds. Both came from deeply religious families; they just naturally hoped that their firstborn would be a preacher.

"It was plain to see that Billy Frank sure wasn't cut out to be a farmer. That's for sure," said Mr. Graham. "How that boy loved to have fun, though! When he was about ten we got him a little goat. Wildest critter you ever saw. Someone once commented as to how odd it was the goat and our boy had the same name, and I reckoned there wasn't a lot of difference between the goat and the boy. He'd hop on his wheel and scoot into the woods with a couple of colts and his hound dog. The goat'd be right on his trail. Billy would hide out in the brush and hoot and holler, and that goat'd have it the craziest time ketchin' him. He was a great one for jokin' and talkin' and generally carryin' on. I figured he'd wind up as a salesman of some kind. Myself, I'd always wanted to be a preacher, but I guess the good Lord just wanted me to be a farmer. Some folks say Billy Frank looks like me—we're both six feet and two inches tall. But if you were to hear him talk, you'd just know the Lord had different jobs cut out for us."

Billy was not a bad student, but he never allowed his studies to disturb the fun he was always engaged in. Once his teacher came home to report that Billy had led her a merry chase around the room, trying to avoid getting his knuckles rapped for a classroom prank. The Grahams did not exactly worry; when he wasn't fooling, he did read a great deal. Much of his literary curiosity involved the Tarzan series; his whoops the morning he tried swinging from branch to branch on the big chestnut tree in front of the house indicated accurately what he had been reading the night before.

What did worry the family was his almost demonic energy. That, combined with his bag-of-bones frame, they were sure would precipitate a physical calamity. But the doctor assured them that his energy was a gift of God, and there was nothing anybody could do about it for better or worse. The boy was never sick; he kept on thriving.

The solidity of the Graham household held him down for daily moments of devotion, when each of the four children would take his turn reading a bit of Scripture. In Calvinist tradition, everybody sang the Psalms; hymns were never heard at the Graham home until the children were in their teens. The Young People's Group of the Chalmers Memorial Associate Reformed Presbyterian Church, where his father was an elder, elected Billy its ranking vice president. If that exalted position and the interest he manifested in the conversation of the traveling revivalists who were boarded free in the Graham household indicated that he might eventually turn to a profession of religion, no one in his family recognized it.

As he looks back on those days, Graham decides that "he must have been getting a reckless attitude on life." He comes to this conclusion now by computing his transgressions: He attended the movies too much. (Mrs. Graham quietly discouraged her children from "such foolishness.") He liked the girls and Mrs. Graham recalled that they were strongly attracted to his easygoing extroverted personality. What really sticks in Billy's memory are the bizarre nights when he and Grady Wilson, his boyhood chum, would borrow Mr. Graham's Plymouth sedan and speed down the main street of Charlotte at midnight, blowing the horn at bootleggers they recognized, hoping to stir up a ruckus.

Although they seldom scolded him, his parents knew he was about ready for serious religious counsel. Mordecai Ham, a persuasive and popular gospel revivalist, had announced his plan to visit Charlotte for a three-month revival campaign. The Grahams, old friends of the evangelist, thought that this was to be the time. A responsive son, Billy agreed to attend the meeting when his mother asked him to. For protection, he took his pal Grady along.

"We sat 'way up there in the balcony—about as far away as we could get," Grady says. "We ducked behind a lady who wore a nice big old floppy hat. At the end of the most blistering sermon I ever heard, old Doc Ham gave the invitation for anybody to come forward and give himself to Christ. He said, 'You up there, you know who you are. You're sinners, and if you don't come now you may suffer eternal damnation.' Honest, so help me, I thought someone had tipped him off on us. Billy looked at me and I looked at him. I think we were both crying. We ran down those steps and knelt in front of old Doc Ham, and right then and there we were saved."

Graham frequently refers meaningfully to this moment as

the "first big decision of my life." He talks about how "the trees and the grass and the flowers all looked different the next day. Everything seemed bright and fresh."

His friends and his family noticed the change. He suddenly became aware of a purpose in his life, attempting to translate his new faith into daily action.

Early one morning he finished his daily milking (twenty cows), then took the milk-delivery truck out. A tire blew. It was 5 A.M., and the mechanic who struggled with it swore a few times. Even in his preconversion period, Billy had not been inclined to swear, but swearing on the part of others had never seriously disturbed him. This morning, however, he bristled like an Elijah in the presence of evil.

"Sir," he said, "do not take my Lord's name in vain."

"I'll do as I damn please, and what do you think you're going to do about it?" the mechanic answered, and swore again at the tire.

"You'll not take my Lord's name in vain," said Graham.

The mechanic picked up a jack handle and swung it a few times under the boy's nose. Billy, white-faced, stood his ground.

"Sir, if you keep on using that language," he said, "I'll have to tell my father, W. F. Graham, to take his business elsewhere."

Graham, who today detests the idea of threatening anybody into behaving virtuously, got his way. It was one of his first battles with evil, and for a long time he was secretly proud of his victory.

Like any new convert, Graham was swimming deep in the river. His conversion created an abyss within him; it pained him that he knew so little about his faith. Every spare night he and Grady would search out revival meetings, prayer meetings or Bible classes. "About that time," he says, "I began my lifetime ambition of studying the Bible so hard that I would know it by heart before I died."

The pastoral calm of the farm couldn't quench his compulsive desire to keep moving. During the summer of 1935 a friend of the family who was the regional manager for the Fuller Brush Company offered to take Billy and Grady on a door-to-door selling expedition through the Carolinas. The Grahams agreed that it might be a good idea to let their son work off some steam by seeing another part of the world. The manager fitted him out with a case of brushes and a boxful of samples, free to the customer but costing Billy a couple of cents apiece.

"Just to get the brush," Grady Wilson says nostalgically, "most of them would let us in. Sometimes they'd let us talk and we'd each slip in a little bit of a sermon just to round things out. At least half the time they'd take the sample, and as soon as we started with the message—business or religious—they'd slam the door in our faces and tell us to get the blazes out of there. Now, brother, that was sure a test of your Christian patience. Never seemed to bother Billy. You just couldn't stop that fella. Later, when we held meetings in those areas and the local chairman would welcome us real flowery-like, I'd look at Billy and he'd smile and say, 'I wonder how many of those good folks in the audience were the same ones that slammed the door in our noses.'"

The summer session benefited Graham greatly. He made more money selling brushes than any of the other fledgling hucksters, and at the same time he experienced the baptism that missionaries of all callings, religious or business, must undergo—overcoming the corrosive effects of the hostility of those who refuse to listen.

That fall, vaguely convinced that his life must somehow center around religion, Graham entered Bob Jones College, then located in Cleveland, Tennessee. The school, a rigidly fundamentalist institution, throbbed with a revivalist spirit; its founder, Bob Jones, Sr., a beloved veteran of the revivalist trial, had coined a colorful slogan for it: "We not only teach our preacher boys how to load the gospel gun, we also teach them to fire it." The flaming spirit of the place defeated the boy. He was too recently a convert from an easygoing secular environment to fit into the pietistic world of Bob Jones. His gospel gunnery was dreadful, and when he quit, three months later, no official at the school seriously considered him much of a loss to the Protestant fellowship.

The following semester, still troubled about his future, Graham enrolled at Temple Terrace Independent Bible School, later Trinity College, in Tampa, Florida. His reasons for going there seemed conflicting, but they were nevertheless understandable. At nineteen, he wanted to get far away from home. Florida sounded romantic. Also, two years at the Institute would ground him well in the Scriptures. While this process unfolded, he suffered a shock that was almost inevitable to a nineteen-year-old, but nonetheless painful. Beneath soft tropical skies he fell in love.

The young lady, a student at the Institute, approached faith and her future with probity. She wanted to marry. She hoped the man that won her would be a clergyman, but, above all, he must show promise of amounting to something. And in her well-ordered opinion, William Franklin Graham, Jr., showed no such promise.

Graham took the blow hard. Sick with failure and shame, he tore into the Florida swamps to nurse his misery. On the muddy banks of the Hillsboro River he begged God for help in resolving the discords of his life. "If you think I should preach, Lord, please make me know it," he once prayed. And one evening he received his answer. From then on, Graham never suffered any doubts about his calling.

Even when he was a child, his voice had a sweet fluidity. He spoke more rapidly than most Southerners and with less of the drawl that characterizes the mountain people in the Piedmont region. Nightly, to practice projecting his ideas, he would walk alone in the swamp and, using a gnarled cypress branch for a lectern, talk out over the swamp waters at the wildlife. He began reading about the challenging world of the Christian evangelist, especially that of Dwight L. Moody, who, with his song leader, Ira D. Sankey, rekindled Protestantism's banked fires of faith during the late nineteenth century with his powerful pulpiteering. Graham decided to pattern his pulpit personality on Moody's; after a semester of swampland polemics he felt that he was getting close.

Grady Wilson, the associate pastor and court jester of the Graham team, used to draw a laugh from team members whenever he related his adventure of searching out Graham at a Florida church where his friend was supposed to be preaching. He described the church, accessible only by mule, swamp boat and Indian guide, as a ramshackle log cabin. And when he reached it at sundown, after an all-day safari, he found only a couple of corncob-smoking, barefooted characters, snoozing against the rotting logs. Neither of them had ever heard of Billy Graham.

Actually Graham's early preaching sessions occurred in places vaguely resembling the one Wilson describes. He also preached at trailer camps in the mud, and bartenders hustled him out of saloons when he ventured there to save a soul. At the end of two years at Trinity he had served a rounded internship in pulpit technique. He was about ready for some good secular education.

At Trinity, Graham's interest in a broad nondenominational Christianity developed. He preached then as he does now—a simple noncreedal Bible message devoid of the constricting bounds of the higher, more liturgical churches. It became difficult for him to fit himself into the disciplined creedalism of the Presbyterian Church; if he was to become an evangelist, the free-wheeling approach of the Baptist fellowship was more nearly suited to his needs. He wrote his parents that he would, with their consent, become a Baptist. They gave him their blessings, but they remained active Presbyterians.

It was a decision Graham never regretted. His primary task as he interprets it—as an evangelist or as a revivalist—is simply to spread the gospel.

" 'Revival' is an Old Testament term," he explains. "The revivalist's job is to rebuild faith in the already converted whose spirits need a lift. 'Evangelism' is a New Testament term. It means bringing Christ's message to the unconverted."

Whether he's preaching to the converted or to the unconverted, Graham never concerns himself with doctrinal quarrels. It makes no difference to him whether one kneels or refuses to kneel; he cares relatively little whether the Communion consists of grape juice or wine; forensics involving infant versus adult baptism play no part in his message; arguments as to whether the taking of the wafer and wine involve the real or the symbolic body of Christ should be resolved, he believes, within the heart of the individual and in schools of divinity; he hopes that churches will unite, but he seldom plunges into the debates on this issue. His only enemy is sin.

In 1940 he enrolled at Wheaton College in Wheaton, Illinois, where Grady was already entered. Wheaton is a nondenominational school no less proud of its fervid religious spirit than of its high academic standing as a liberal arts college. It frequently has been the scene of marathon student revivals that have lasted through the night and into the following day.

Here too Graham won no scholastic honors, but the intellectual atmosphere of Wheaton, unlike anything he had known before, stimulated his inner resources. On the campus he was accorded special respect for his precollege preaching credits. His classmates elected him president of the Christian Council, the highest honor a Wheaton undergraduate can achieve. The president of the school named him student pastor of the campus church. Solid pews of Ph.D.s as well as of schoolmates spurred him to careful research efforts in preparing his sermons.

One of the regular attendants at his services was Ruth Bell, a pretty, brown-eyed coed who had recently returned with her parents from China, where Dr. L. Nelson Bell served as a Presbyterian medical missionary. Graham met her one hot day when he lugged her heavy trunk to her room. Later, after he had learned a little about her, he remarked admiringly to Grady, "Boy, I hear that girl prays at least three times a day." They double-dated with Grady Wilson and Ruth's friend Wilma, also undergraduates, and had many laughs together over thick chocolate malts at the local ice-cream parlor.

"Billy was a barrel of fun. And Ruth never tired of kidding him in her 'servant' Chinese. But whether he was kidding—he was a real tease—or serious, there was no doubt in our minds that Billy would do something big in his lifetime," Wilma Wilson says.

Shortly after graduation Billy and Ruth married. Their first pastorate was a few miles outside of Chicago, the Village Baptist Church in Western Springs, Illinois. The entire congregation of thirty-five souls marched into the basement church to welcome the new pastor. To create interest in his church and to obtain the financial support necessary to outfit it with a main floor and a steeple, which it lacked, Graham whipped up the idea of a religious radio program. Its minimum budget was estimated at $150 a week; the whole church functioned on $85 a week. Graham did something then that has since won him admiration in the Protestant fellowship: he took the church problem to Christian businessmen in the community. That, he figured, was a matter for good business heads to handle; more important, the move served to get individuals with local authority and prestige involved in church affairs as they had never been involved before. Graham is still a great believer in that tactic today; he makes dozens of speeches annually before businessmen's groups, stimulating compliance with the Biblical injunction to tithe—to give at least ten percent of one's income to the church.

Graham and his Western Springs deacons elicited support from their community and then prayed for their radio ministry. After a season of such preparation they went on the air with a program called "Songs in the Night." Beverly Shea and a girls' quartet sang. Graham delivered a four-minute sermonette.

In Chicago in those days, a jet-propelled young preacher named Torrey Johnson was forming Youth for Christ, an evangelistic movement to counteract the growing wave of delinquency among young people. Johnson heard Graham on the radio and realized that here was exactly the kind of young people's preacher he had been looking for. They became good friends. Johnson asked Graham to resign his pulpit and go on the road for Youth for Christ. Before accepting, Graham prayed.

"I read Ephesians again and again," he recounts, "where it mentions that the Lord gave some to be evangelists and some to be pastors. God just did not want for me to be a pastor."

He traveled across the country and back so many times that he can hardly remember the towns he visited. His salary was $300 a month; to hold expenses down, he frequently traveled by auto, and he lived in third-class hotels like a small-time vaudevillian on tour.

At a Bible Conference stopover he met Cliff Barrows, a young people's preacher and song leader who by this time had seen as much of the country as Graham. Barrows, a genial man four years younger than Graham, has a sweet, warm personality. At Bob Jones College he majored in ministerial music, knowing even then that he wanted to become an evangelist song leader. His great hero was the legendary Homer Rodeheaver, who toured the country with Billy Sunday in his colorful revival crusades during the early part of the century.

Barrows and Graham sprang from similar home backgrounds. Barrows' parents were deeply devout fruit farmers in Modesto, California, and they too had prayed that their firstborn would be a minister. In high school his classmates called him "Preacher." Once his colleagues in the school band conspired to trick him into joining them in a jive session. Beneath his "Pomp and Circumstance" music they slipped the sheets of "The St. Louis Blues." The band finished the first piece, then without warning skidded into the jazz. Barrows' eyes widened; he dropped his trombone and stalked out of the hall.

Wherever Barrows and Graham traveled, they were met with an enthusiasm that grew from year to year. The audiences grew in numbers, and requests for their services began coming from older groups.

"At first that surprised me," Barrows says. "I'd always thought our work was strictly for the younger folks. But not Billy.

He was always reading about current events—he got every news magazine, listened to all the political speeches on the radio—and he kept saying there was a powerful demand for religion. Said he just could feel there was a great revival coming—but fast—to this country."

Between 1946 and 1949, Graham and Barrows made six trips to Europe, participating in Youth for Christ international conventions and preaching through interpreters. The vigor and optimism of Graham's personality captivated an aged but still fiery revivalist named W. B. Riley, who operated The Northwestern Schools, a glorified Bible institute in Minneapolis. Riley sought out the young preacher. Like a prophet of old, Riley informed Graham that he must assume the leadership of the school when he himself died. On his deathbed in 1947 Riley repeated his instructions.

At the time Graham was busily campaigning all over the world. He explained to the school trustees that he did not feel up to the challenge, but that he honestly did not dare reject the wishes of the old man. He agreed to take the job on the condition that he would continue his evangelistic work. By any yardstick, it was one of the strangest of college presidencies. Graham ran the school by long-distance telephone. Before he relinquished its leadership in 1951, he had secured for it a new building and, more important, academic accreditation.

During the early days of his ministry, after he left Youth for Christ, Graham and his teammates drew their incomes from "love offerings" taken up for them at the end of each crusade. Sensitive to the criticism surrounding too many gospel revivalists, who blew into town with a message and left it with a pocketful of local currency, Graham determined that the dignity of his mission would never be so sullied. He organized the Billy Graham Evangelical Association, a nonprofit organization, supported by voluntary contributions. The Association, run by a board of directors, handles the business side of Graham's many ventures, including his books, films and columns. All profits go into the Association's coffers. The Association pays all salaries of the team.

In his Minneapolis headquarters, which Graham seldom visits, 205 paid employees mail out millions of pieces of Graham-written or inspired religious literature annually, including the magazine *Decision*. His radio and TV program "Hour of Decision" is paid for entirely by listeners.

None of the staggering costs of the Billy Graham Evangelical Association comes directly from the proceeds of a local crusade. Graham asks only that the running expenses of the team be paid while they are in town. No other money is accepted. He also insists that all funds from a crusade be publicly audited and published. "I learned a long time ago," he says, "how to stifle any personal interest in money. It is just no problem. And it need not be for any Christian."

Since the demand for his services has become so insistent and universal, Graham's organization bases its choices of places to be visited upon these standards: the need of the community for Graham's services and the number of churches that extend the invitation. In these last years his work has become so firmly connected with the churches in the communities he has visited that now he hesitates to go into a community unless all or almost all of the Protestant churches there ask for the crusade. He has been laboring (without much success) to separate his personality from his crusades, to make the crusades expressive of church dynamism rather than of the personality of a pulpiteer.

As the country's most renowned evangelist, Graham is always having to provide a reasonable answer to the question of how long a conversion lasts when it is made in the heat of a camp-meeting atmosphere. Graham has a stock response to the question. He borrows Billy Sunday's famous answer: "A bath doesn't last long, does it? But is that any argument against taking one?"

But Graham, a man who feels his responsibilities deeply, realizes that the "decisions," as he prefers to call them, must surpass the character of quick ablution, or his mission will fail. And so his organization sends out full-time follow-up men to check up on the converts. It is a very difficult job. As soon as Graham leaves a town, the churches are once again in full command, as

Graham fervently believes they should be. Frequently these churches have little reason to be as statistically minded as Graham's organization, and getting accurate figures is a laborious business. But, so far as he can determine, at least 40 percent of those who declare their willingness to become Christians at one of his meetings are active church members six months later.

In the last couple of years Graham and his teammates have worried less about the number of converts than about the kind of lives they lead after they make their decisions. The traditional point of view of the free-lance revivalist was embodied in the words of one who said: "My job is to shake them with a fear of the Almighty and dazzle them with His love. Just make them repent; the rest will take care of itself."

In his early preaching days Graham limited himself generally to this function. But gradually he has broadened his ministry; he preaches the two virtues of Christian living: one, the vertical relationship of the individual with God; two, the horizontal relationship of the Christian with his fellowman, necessitating the doing of good works and the embracing of what is known as the social gospel. An individual who accepts one and rejects the other is only half a Christian, Graham believes, "and you can't really be that."

During the recent New York World's Fair, Graham took advantage of the exposure potentialities of the exhibition. The Association built a Billy Graham pavilion where a film was shown and where thousands came to secure aid and comfort administered by dozens of volunteer counselors.

The keystone of Graham's faith is fixed within the attitude he and the followers of "the old-time religion" affect toward Jesus. In this atmosphere the Savior comes to the individual believer not through an ordained priesthood or via the good office of a specially enlightened human with a special pipeline to God; the faithful come to know the Lord through personal experience. This form of simple Protestantism, devoid of intellectual entwinings, laboriously constructed creeds and a custodial clergy, is basically an easily available, personal religion.

"It is," says Archie Robertson in his charming book *That Old Time Religion,* "Protestant Christianity with . . . belief in the right of the individual to interpret the Bible according to his own conscience . . . in religious liberty . . . and especially . . . in the ability of each soul to deal directly with its Creator. . . . The institutions of the old time religion are not holy or sacred to its followers, in the sense that Catholic institutions are sacred to a Catholic. They are open to self-criticism."

Graham reveres the freedom that this type of religion embodies. But humor surrounding the church and religious matters he finds hard to take. Darkly, he charges that it "has become fashionable to joke about the Bible." People were using it, he adds, as a repository for old flowers and sweet-smelling letters. And as for those who treat the Bible as a magnificent volume of history, or the best codebook for ethics, or as fine poetry, and pay no attention to its message of human redemption, the best Graham can say is that they are guilty of the sin of disbelief.

For many intellectuals, the Bible is this kind of book. It is they, according to Graham, who are always rewriting the truths in the Bible instead of accepting the words exactly as they are.

"We can ask the learned scholars and they may tell us that God is the expression of everything that is in nature and life. . . . Ask a philosopher and he will tell you that God is the original and immutable force behind all creation. . . . Ask still further and you may be told that God is absolute, that He is All in All, and that no one can possibly know more about Him. . . . Which of these varied explanations are we to believe? God reveals himself in hundreds of ways in the Bible, and if we read the Bible as carefully as we read the daily papers, we would be as familiar with and as well informed about God as we are about our favorite player's batting average during baseball season."

On the platform Graham seldom takes direct issue with those who treat of God as a force, as everything in nature, or anything other than a very real personal creature in Whose image He made man. It is part of Graham's conviction as an evangelist that some of these more specific points are diversions from his main thesis—the urgent need for man to repent before his God, no matter what His exact form might take in the mind of the convert. But in Graham's book *Peace with God,* he spells out his own convictions on the subject, dotting the *i*'s and crossing the *t*'s with sure strokes. He conceives of God, as it says in the Bible, as Spirit.

"If you have been trying to limit God, stop it," he adjures. "You wouldn't try to limit the ocean. You wouldn't be bold enough to try to change the course of the moon, or to stop the earth as it turns on its axis! The Bible reveals Him as a person. A person is one who feels, thinks, wishes, desires, and has all the expressions of personality. . . . God is not bound by a body, yet He is a Person."

In explaining the meaning of sin, Graham, glued to his literal beliefs, returns to the primary source—the book of Genesis. Adam was no symbol, the Garden of Eden no imaginary bit of real estate. God, he contends, created an absolutely perfect world, in which he placed an absolutely perfect man. Although he was an anthropology major in college, Graham rejects the Darwinian concept of natural selection and evolution as it pertains to man. The theory satisfies him insofar as animal life is concerned. But the first man was not, he says, a "jibbering, grunting, growling creature of the forest trying to subdue the perils of the jungle and the beasts of the field. Adam was created full-grown, with every mental and physical faculty developed, a perfect man in His own likeness. . . . Adam was the fountainhead of the human race." Stretching to heights of rhetoric, Graham intones that Adam "sprang like a crystal-clear spring from the ground and was permitted to choose whether he would become a river running through pleasant and productive green pastures, or a muddy torrent forever dashing against rocks and churning between deep, sunless cliffs—cold and miserable in itself, and unable to bring joy and fruitfulness to the surrounding land."

Graham refers to Adam as the "federal head of the human race." Because he disobeyed God's instructions in the Garden of Eden and tasted of the fruit, he fell from God's grace and has been dragging the human race with him ever since. Before his error Adam had available to him all the goodness of life without care. Once fallen, man must "toil all the days of his life to provide these necessities for himself and his family. Woman, once the most carefree of creatures, is now burdened with sorrow and pain; and both men and women are under penalty of spiritual and physical death."

No matter how hard we try—no matter how good we may consider our deportment on this earth—we cannot, says Graham, escape this earthly punishment. Graham warns that it will do no good for man to attempt to make light of sin or to call it by sweeter-sounding names. Man has no right to call sin an accident or treat it as a minor matter. It is "no amusing toy," warns Graham. "It is a terror to be shunned." And God, in convicting man of it, sent his only begotten son, Jesus, to earth so that man might have the means to redeem himself from the catastrophe that befell him.

The only thing that will shut the door to heaven and shove man into the holocaust of hell is his refusal to believe this, Graham holds. When some who do not easily accept these solemn pronouncements ask Graham what will happen to those millions who live by other articles of faith, such as the Koran, the Buddhist scriptures, the Brahman Vedas, the Zoroastrian Zend-Avesta, and the Hebrew Talmud, Graham replies sadly but insistently that these people, by not accepting the True Word, must someday pay the eternal penalty. For those who cannot read or who have never been exposed to the Truth, Graham admits he does not have the answer. "God," he says, "has a place for those people."

Adam, the devil, the Garden of Eden, and hell are no less real than heaven to Graham. Some scholars, he points out, have tried to indicate that heaven is someplace north. Graham admits to no geographical knowledge of the Celestial City, but he is positive that it exists as a very real place where Christ is. The Bible, he claims, tells him that it is a region where grand reunions will take place; people who met and separated on earth will meet each other all over again. Only there will all the heartaches and tragedies of life be resolved forevermore, and all the wondering we do about eternal creation will be cleared up for everybody once and for all. He does not expect that we will just loll around in chairs of spun gold and listen to good music. "The Bible indicates that . . . there will be work to do for God. We will spend much time praising Him. . . . It will be a time of joy, service, laughter and singing and praise to God." Not only will we be raised in spirit, but, Graham feels, we will be recreated in body.

"Scientists have already proved," Graham says, "that no chemicals disappear from the earth. The God who made the body in the first place can bring all the original chemicals back together again and the body will be raised to join the soul. But the new body we will have will be a glorious body like unto the body of Christ. It will be an eternal body."

By the same token, Graham is sure that the sinners—those who refused on this earth to believe—will live in an entirely contrasting kind of world. He does not know what exact form it will take, but he is positive that it will be simply awful.

In his theology Graham does not neglect the social obligation of the Christian. Leaving the convert no choice, Graham proclaims that the Christian *must* "be concerned with social problems and social injustices. . . . Child labor has been outlawed, slavery has been abolished. The status of women has been lifted . . . as a result of the influence of the teachings of Jesus Christ. . . . Christians should be interested in orphanages, hospitals, asylums, prisons and all social institutions."

On the matter of sex, normally a gloomy subject for most revivalists, Graham speaks out. "Sex, the act by which all life on this earth is created, should be the most wonderful, the most meaningful, the most satisfying of human experiences. Man with his vile self-destructive nature . . . has made it low and cheap and filthy. The sly, secret, embarrassed let's-pretend-it-doesn't-exist attitude about sex is purely man-made. . . . Nowhere does the Bible teach that sex itself is a sin, although many interpreters of the Bible would try to make it appear so. . . . Used rightly it can bring heaven into the home."

On the subject of labor relations: "The Bible teaches there is dignity in all types of honest labor. . . . The Christian employer should be concerned about safety precautions, good working conditions. . . . He will not only see his workers as 'man power' but also as human beings. . . . Social liberty for the working classes began when a Christian leader, Lord Shaftesbury . . . led a lifelong crusade for better conditions . . . for the working man."

Graham does not see extreme asceticism as having any special divine purpose. "Too many Christians have taken a most sinful and damaging pride in being poverty stricken, in standing by helplessly and saying, 'God's will be done,' as their children suffered and went untended."

It disturbs Graham that Christians quarrel among themselves and that each sect insists that it alone has the correct answer and is therefore quick to condemn the others.

"To be sure, we must deplore what we consider wickedness, evil and wrongdoing," he once stated. "But our commendable intolerance of sin too often develops into a deplorable intolerance of sinners."

A Southerner, Graham admits to a sense of responsible shame when he contemplates the race problem in the South. "The Church has failed in solving this great human problem. We have let the sports world, the entertainment field, politics, the armed services, education and industry outstrip us. The Church should have been a pace setter. The churches should be voluntarily doing what the federal courts are doing by pressure. . . . When Christ opens our spiritual eyes we behold not color or class . . . but simply human beings with the same longings, fears, needs and aspirations as our own."

Once while he was conducting a campaign in the South, a reporter asked him whether he saw a justification for segregation in the Bible. Graham snapped, "Absolutely none."

Because of this unseemly liberalism from one they consider their own, some arch-fundamentalists display occasional irritation with Graham, associating him with "those backsliding modernists." Actually Graham, with his conviction that "evolution is all right for animals but all wrong for people," is in no danger of becoming a theological liberal.

He gets a buffeting from extremists at both ends of the religious scale for not taking a firm stand on one side of the line and publicly rejecting everything on the other side. Caught in the middle, Graham protests that evangelists, cutting across all heterogeneous groups, *must not* create artificial barriers in this way. A pastor who is responsible to one homogeneous group, on the other hand, *must* take a strong position, he believes. "I know, for example," he says, "that many people come to our meetings with profound convictions against the type of conversion they see there. I respect their convictions and would not want them to change because of me. But we leave the door open to them. If I denounced their point of view, as some of my well-meaning friends would want me to, I would drive them out and split an evangelistic campaign asunder."

After the arduous schedules of his crusades, Graham returns home to renew acquaintance with his wife and the three children who are at home (one is married), and to refurbish his energies.

Their home is located in Montreat, North Carolina, in the colorful foothills of the Blue Ridge Mountains, smack in the middle of the Presbyterian Bible Conference grounds. It has become something of a local shrine. The people feel a strong personal possessiveness about Graham, and wander in the environs of his hill house with the freedom of a congregation visiting the local parsonage.

At the top of the mountain, Graham, now forty-eight, blends into the verdure as naturally as a farm boy should. In T-shirt and jeans, his insistent boyishness is accentuated. His face is long and his chin is deeply chiseled, so that his jaw gives the appearance of jutting forward. He has heard himself described as "falcon-faced." It used to irritate him a little; now, after millions of descriptive words have been written about him, he is impervious to any personal description. His skin stays a satiny white until the summer sun hits it, and then it warms to a soft amber. He searches the face of anyone with whom he speaks—neighbor or church official or stranger—with the same direct intensity, his blue eyes shining alertly.

Graham's only magic formula for keeping his skinny frame from rattling itself apart under the pressure of his corrosive schedule is to sleep more than most people. At home he gets to bed around ten-thirty and is up about eight. He comes downstairs in his pajamas to sit down to an early breakfast—one of the five meals he eats on an average day.

In his study he pours sermons and ideas into a Dictaphone, and later he is joined by his wife. Ruth Graham is as bright-eyed now as the day they married. Graham reveres her good sense; when they were stuck for a title for the radio program, it was she who suggested "Hour of Decision."

To people who ask her the old question about what it's like to be married to a man who is home so little, she answers, looking at him warmly, "I'd rather see a little of him than a lot of anybody else."

She is adept at giving him an idea for a sermon and then gliding out of his study so that he can work it over. He dictates his sermons in rough outline. He has no need for a prepared script for any message; with an outline, his natural Southern fluidity and his rich familiarity with the Bible, he speaks easily in any situation.

After a few hours in his study, Billy hops out of the house restlessly, perhaps to walk the hills or run off for a round of golf with a few of his old local friends. A healthy, extroverted type, Graham has little desire to shut himself in a study for too long. Intellectualism is not his forte. He recognizes that this period in history demanded revival; he believes God gave him a job to do, and he is doing it as best he can. He doesn't honestly feel that he will be called upon to do it much longer. "The world will either see the light or go up in smoke." In either case, he humbly considers he will be expendable.

JIMMY KARAM

Violence Converted to Love

IF A Hollywood producer were doing a movie on the life of Jimmy Karam, he'd have no trouble casting the star role. It would be a natural for Jimmy Cagney because the part calls for a short, pugnacious brawler who slugs his way into politics, position and prominence.

The clichés are all there—poverty to riches, girls, gambling, the first-generation son forcing anguish upon gentle, God-fearing parents. And then follows the traditional cinema denouement— the spiritual rebirth converting infamy to applause, rage to love, all inspired by an inner redemption resulting from a discovery and acceptance of God and the Christian message.

A typical scene in the picture might take place in Little Rock, Arkansas. It's an election year and Governor Orval Faubus is running for a third term in office. Although the Governor is a favorite to win the election, he's not having the easiest time of it. For one thing, the labor unions, the liberals, the moderates are mustering strength against him. For another, the Negro, aided by federal law and national sympathy, is growing restive, aggressively demanding his civil rights. And Governor Faubus—a shrewd man and a shrewder politician—is taking no chances. He calls his aide-de-camp, Jimmy Karam.

"It isn't that I have any doubts about winning, Jimmy," the Governor tells him, "I want to win big."

Jimmy nods. "Sure, I know, Governor. Nothing like a landslide to show up those damn Yankees, burn their fingers a little and make them think twice about sticking them in this cookie jar." And then Jimmy adds, "Don't give it another thought, Governor. I'll take care of things."

The scene dissolves to Jimmy Karam's headquarters in Little Rock, where he is surrounded by ten of his "boys."

"All we have tonight, fellers, is two little jobs," he says with a sly smile. "That integration meetin' downtown and the agitatin' at the church where the niggers are now singin' up a storm. We've got to do a little mussin' up to discourage them a little."

The "boys" know his language and they know how to work. They move swiftly, force doors, drag the leaders from the platform, swinging fists and clubs, smashing, cursing and threatening with forceful efficiency. Police arrive conspicuously late. Arrests, for "lack of evidence," are seldom made. The leader, the chunky barrel-chested man with the mended nose, is seldom close by. The "general" remains at headquarters, frequently the state capitol. Here, he receives communiqués from the street battles, and barks new strategy orders. Again Jimmy Karam and his goons have broken the opposition—literally. And again Governor Faubus wins by a landslide.

So much for our mythical Hollywood spectacular in blood-red color and wide-eyed VistaVision. Despite the Hollywood trappings, most of it is true. This is the Jimmy Karam that was. But how did he get that way? And how did he get where he is now?

To answer these questions we have to go back to the year 1904. It was then that Jimmy Karam's Armenian parents journeyed from Lebanon in the Middle East to visit the St. Louis World's Fair. The Karams liked so much of what they saw in the New World, they decided to stay. But not in St. Louis. The climate was too harsh for them. They moved south to the gentler weather of Mississippi. They settled near the town of Greenville, where the elder Karam started his New World business career with a pack on his back, peddling dry goods from door to door. The enterprising immigrant trudged long days along the dusty back roads, saved, and eventually opened a store in Lake Village, Arkansas, 120 miles from Little Rock. Here Jimmy Karam was born in 1912.

"I guess you never know how important your birthplace is," Jimmy Karam says. "If I was born in, say, Jersey City, chances are I'd never even know who Faubus was. Not that I'm blaming the Governor, mind you. What I did was all me, not him. Nobody *made* me do anything. I'm sure the devil lives in Jersey City just as he lives in Little Rock."

Although, as Jimmy Karam says, the devil can live anywhere, the fact remains that Arkansas provided a combination of elements that made him what he was and what he is. A foreigner in the deep South is more of a foreigner than he is in the melting pot of the North; the Negro problem in the deep South was more volatile than in the Midwest; and politics in the South was more incestuous than in any other part of the nation.

Jimmy Karam's parents were almost one-of-a-kind foreigners in Lake Village, Arkansas. The "better people" in the town tolerated them, most others abused them or shunned them. In a remote way stop such as Lake Village, few knew what a Lebanese was. So the Karams were "Greeks," "Wops," or just plain "furriners." Although the elder Karam had done well as a peddler, his store was not a bonanza. It was one thing to buy an occasional bargain item from an itinerant peddler; quite another to become a steady customer of a foreigner's establishment.

A local police officer or two, aware of the "furriner's" defenselessness, "bought" on credit, picking out the best and seldom bothering to pay.

"Why do you let them do that to you, Papa?" the indignant young Jimmy would ask. "I don't care if they are the police. It's just plain stealing." His father, steeped in the ghetto ways of the old country with its built-in fear of authority, especially police, would say, "What can I do, Jimmy? I'm afraid of them. We're strangers here. We have to walk on tiptoe. We have no one to turn to."

Bitterly the youngster understood his father's meekness. Not only were the Karams foreigners who spoke with a strange accent, they were also Catholic. That combination in the South was, in some respects, even more damning than being a Negro. An "uppity" Catholic "furriner" in the rural South could rightly be afraid of a night visit from the Klan with results that might range from a cross burning to a store burning. And, as his father had said, there was no one to turn to.

But if Jimmy Karam's father was holding his breath as he tiptoed through life, Jimmy Karam was breathing hard. It was as though he were compensating for his father's fear. As he grew older, the chip on his shoulder grew bigger.

"I didn't take any lip from anybody," he says, remembering his earlier days. "Just let anyone make a crack about me or my folks—where they came from or how they talked funny—and I'd push a fist in his mouth that would shut him up, but good and tight."

With his stone-hard body, swiveling on muscled hips, and his short powerful legs, he resembled a Dixie Mickey Walker, the prizefighter they called the "Toy Bulldog." Every inch of him was tough and fearless. He took them, big or small, as they came, cutting each down to size.

Young Jimmy Karam's way of life wasn't calculated to win friends but it certainly influenced people. If they didn't like him, they feared him. He said then, that was enough for him . . . but it wasn't, really. Deep down, his desire was to be loved and respected, but it was so deep down it couldn't struggle up to the top for air. Besides, then it would have been a weakness to admit it even to himself.

"I wanted the nice people in town to like me. They just never did," he explains. "I guess I never knew why and acted as though I didn't give a damn."

It was only natural for Jimmy Karam the schoolboy to gravitate to the highly competitive sport of football. He also went in for track and field, concentrating on the 100- and the 220-yard dash. But track was only incidental; what it did was to perfect his speed for the real game on the gridiron. He played high-school football at St. Barnabas, a Catholic school in Mississippi, and he was so good at it that Alabama's Auburn College offered him a football scholarship in 1937. He took it and carried the ball hard enough and far enough to be nominated for All-American recognition. He was a missile of football fury and to this day fans who watched him play tell about him with awe.

"Loved football," he says. "Nothing like running down the field with the ball, stiff-arming all those beefy lugs out of my way—or making a flying tackle that brings a 200-pound halfback down on his nose."

He thinks about it a minute; shakes his head over it. "Now, when I watch a fight or a football game on TV, it's all different somehow. I watch one boxer beating another one to a pulp, and I say to myself, 'That man could have the devil in him, just the way I had.' And I feel sorry for him even though he's winning the fight. Today I'm separated from violence. It's something I keep suppressing like it's an evil stranger."

After he got out of school, Jimmy Karam went to work for Goodyear. He didn't care too much for the job—Jimmy didn't take kindly to working for anyone—but it gave him enough money to spend on girls, gambling and drinking. He lived from day to day, sowing a farmful of wild oats.

"When you gonna settle down, Jimmy?" his father would ask time and time again; especially after Jimmy had had a big night out.

"Not now, Pop, please. Not this morning. Can't you see I got a hangover?"

"You got a hangover almost every morning, Jimmy. You can't go on this way all the time. You got to start making a decent life for yourself."

The dialogue between father and son was as poignant as it

was familiar. The father pleading for the son to settle down, find a nice girl, get married. The son demanding to be let alone, with the parting concession that he would think about it.

But "making a life for himself" was at worst a small problem for Jimmy Karam. A natural leader, and a born salesman, he made luck as he pursued fortune. Even at the card table or on the track, Jimmy attracted luck as easily as he had plowed through the opposing line on the gridiron. His courage and his swift willingness to act when he was in pursuit of a goal attracted a few less than scrupulous businessmen, who offered him fast riches if he would employ his leadership and his violent ways in smashing efforts of labor-union representatives to organize workers.

But there were times when Jimmy pondered his father's urgings. It was beginning to be time to settle down. In 1940 he gave in, took a wife and went into business for himself. The girl he married was a schoolteacher, a nice girl.

Jimmy Karam's excursion into the respectable life didn't last very long. He settled down with a thud. When he looked around him all he saw was his nice wife, his nice haberdashery store and his nice, dull existence. He was unhappy, restless. He itched for all the good times he used to have. He missed the girls, the drinking and the gambling. It was particularly bad when he happened to run into one of his old cronies. The conversation would turn along these lines:

"Hey, Jimmy-boy, where you hidin' yourself these days?"

"Oh, I been around, Bo," Jimmy says sheepishly.

"Not where anyone can see, you ain't. . . . No bowlin' any more, no pool, no poker at the club. Man, you sure are buckin' for the pearly gates."

"Well, you know how it is, Bo. You get married, settle down. . . ."

His friend Bo laughs. "Not you, Jimmy. Not yet. You're wastin' a lot of livin'. Come on, boy, snap out of it. How about a little pool tonight and a little hell raisin' later on?"

"Thanks, Bo. Not tonight. Maybe some other time."

"Don't wait too long, Jimmy. You'll forget what livin' is."

Jimmy Karam nods and says good-bye.

Those meetings confused him, churned up all the old lusts and hungers. He wanted to be the same old Jimmy Karam again. Even though he walked away from temptation, temptation walked with him. Yet he did his best to put a good face on his new life. His wife and his father and mother may have suspected his restlessness but they couldn't be sure. And while they wondered and worried, Jimmy looked for a way out. Recalling it now, he recognizes that the equipment for success was not yet with him.

"The devil was in me," he says, "and I couldn't shake him loose. If it weren't for my father and mother—my wife didn't matter so much—I would have lit out like I was on fire. I knew it would break their hearts."

In the end, Jimmy Karam's problem was settled for him. It took a Pearl Harbor and a second world war, but these world-shaking events gave him his way out. Before the dust had settled on that "date that will live in infamy," Jimmy was headed for the Navy. He sold his store and left his family with their blessings. For all he knew, he might have been headed for the Philippines or for Okinawa or some other black hole of combat. It didn't matter; just as long as he got away. . . . But the Navy had other plans for Jimmy Karam.

"Couldn't believe it when they put me into Special Services," he says. "Imagine going through World War II coaching Navy football teams. It wasn't my idea of how to beat Germany and Japan but that's the way the brass wanted it. They said it was the best kind of morale-building for the men."

It was also morale-building for Jimmy Karam. Once again he was free to run around, drink it up and gamble to his heart's content. And he could do it all without his family's disapproval. When the war's end came in 1945, Karam was deeply grateful to the Navy. His four-year hitch was well spent. Now he knew for sure how he wanted to live; to please nobody but himself.

This time he didn't go home to Lake Village, Arkansas. He went to Little Rock, and he didn't take his wife with him. As far as Jimmy was concerned, his marriage was finished and he wasn't going to take too long to make it official. The first thing Jimmy did was get a job as football coach for Little Rock Junior College. Then he opened a high-powered men's haberdashery store in town. He knew both businesses well and he also knew that each would serve the other. His football job—with its accompanying publicity—would bring customers into his clothing store. The clothing customers would return the compliment by attending the college football games. It was a lovely two-way street and Karam collected the tolls coming and going.

"When things go right, they just go right," he says, thinking back to it now. "It was a sweet setup and I made bundles of money as well as being a hero to boot. Of course, it helped some that I did a good job coaching, but I had good tough kids at that school and I showed them how to play rough, winning football. It was no accident that my boys were invited to play in the Little Rose Bowl three years running."

A town like Little Rock makes the most of its local heroes. Football is a fever all over the South and every time the junior-college team played and won, Karam's praises were displayed in gaudy headlines. As a football hero, Karam was "in" before he came to town. He was well remembered as that tough ball carrier from Auburn. It didn't take long for Jimmy to become an even bigger celebrity than before. People knew him wherever he went but, mostly, he went to the right places where he could see the right people. After all, it was more fun to drink with the right people, gamble with the right people and mix it up with the right kind of women than it was to confine your pleasures to the poolroom set. Jimmy became so adept at climbing the ladder of success, he was able to skip a couple of rungs when he neared the top. . . . In that period, the astute Orval Faubus became aware of him. The Governor was impressed by Karam's style. He liked his toughness, his no-nonsense attitude, mostly his brutal drive for results.

Karam's amoral approach to his task, together with the lust for leading forays into action, made him the perfect anti-union goon. He surrounded himself with a coterie of roughneck Hessians, angry discontents who would break a head to order for a fast stipend and never ask a question.

With the objectivity of an observer describing the transgressions of a strangely remote "other" person, he explains how that old Jimmy Karam would disrupt meetings, smash furniture and bodies in a mass scrimmage of violence, even tossing a couple of union organizers out of hotel windows to teach an object lesson administered in the distinctive Karam manner.

"Never hated unions, or those guys," he says ingenuously. "If I were in their place I'd do the same to a goon if he tried to bust up my union. It was money—the devil's kind—and I took it. And in those days it never kept me from sleeping good."

He explains his feelings further. "As far as the Negroes were concerned, I knew how they felt. I knew from firsthand experience what it was to be a minority. Wasn't my family foreign and Catholic? . . . Most people won't believe it, but I never disliked Negroes. Why, when I was coaching the Little Rock team, I let a Negro school use our football field. Some bigots didn't like it. It never stopped me."

Now, thinking back on it, he smiles ruefully. "And if you think I'm not giving you an honest count, you can check with the Urban League in Little Rock. They had me up for head of the organization. I missed it by one vote. . . . Of course, that was before I got in real deep with Faubus and started the rough stuff."

When he got in "real deep" with Faubus (he bossed five gubernatorial campaigns and won them all), Jimmy Karam really came into his own as a human bulldozer. First off, he got rid of his wife—the girl who was "too nice" for him. With his marriage out of the way, he played the field of fillies—human and equine—and he scored all around. Those were the years following the 1954 Supreme Court decision that proclaimed equal rights throughout the land. It was a signal for the powers of reaction to get to work and Jimmy Karam was boss of the work gang.

"We made a shambles of them," he recalls. "By the time we got through with a job, there was nothing left to do but pick up the pieces. . . . When I think back on it now, it scares me. There were only ten men—my goon squad and me—but we could lay everything and everybody low in a matter of minutes. We could have taken over the city if we wanted to."

He says he thinks about it now and then; especially during a catastrophe like the electric-power failure in '65, which immobilized eight states and 80 million people.

"Could have done as good a job—if not better—with my ten goons," he says. "If you have the right kind of men and the right kind of tools—and I *had* them—it's no trick to black out a power system, and cripple the water, oil and gas lines. Violence and destruction come easy to the devil's henchmen. They always do. Much easier to destroy than to build. Very simply, that's the way the Hitlers, Mussolinis and Stalins did it."

It is difficult to equate the Jimmy Karam of today with the Jimmy Karam of ten years ago. Now the man stands quietly in the corner of one of his two smart and successful Little Rock clothing establishments, talking about the old days—the days of violence and bloodshed, when the words "Little Rock" were anathema throughout the civilized world and bore a striking resemblance to a vile curse. Then it was Arkansas and Governor Faubus against the world. At least, that's the way it seemed to the general public. But the insiders knew that Governor Faubus was not alone. He may have been carrying the segregationist ball in the open field but it was the fierce Karam who ran the interference. It was Jimmy Karam who acted as a buffer against the squeeze-play pressures from Washington—the entreating calls from the White House and from the Attorney General. Jimmy just didn't let them go through. He picked up the phone and barked that the Governor was either unavailable or out of town, and that was that.

Perhaps the most notorious and flagrant example of the Karam brand of hooliganism occurred in October, 1957, following the United States Supreme Court's decision that outlawed the "equal but separate" education of the South and ordered the states to integrate their schools forthwith. The focal point was Little

Rock's Central High School. Here, nine Negro children were permitted, with the blessing of the Court, to register at the school, which had heretofore boasted an all-white enrollment of 2,000.

The "threat" of integration in Little Rock was a challenge that Governor Faubus—the then arch-segregationist of the South, eager for the support of the white racists in his bid for a third term in office—couldn't ignore. Knowing the temper of the white citizens of the community, he forecast a bloodbath of violence if the nine Negro children attempted to break the all-white barrier at Central High. In order to avoid this "catastrophe," he would call out the National Guard, with its bayoneted rifles, to thwart the admission of the children and the will of the Court.

This defiant declaration, which was echoed throughout the world—distorted by our enemies, explained by our friends—was answered by President Eisenhower. "Ike" issued a Presidential order which federalized the Arkansas National Guard. In addition, the President instructed Army Chief of Staff Maxwell Taylor to call up the 101st Airborne Division and dispatch it to Little Rock to maintain law and order and implement integration. In the face of this federal show of force, Governor Faubus called off his state militia. But this was only a tactical maneuver. The Governor was relying on his "palace guard" to stir up the little fires of racial hatred and get a real blaze going. The "palace guard," of course, was Jimmy Karam and his hoodlums.

Showdown day for Little Rock—the Monday when the nine Negro children were supposed to enter Central High—began at 6 A.M. Seventy policemen were on hand to keep "law and order." Also on hand was a growing crowd of mean-looking whites, whom the police had permitted to gather instead of dispersing them. And also on hand was Jimmy Karam, who moved through the crowd whispering a word here, an order there, making telephone calls that swelled the ugly mob to almost a thousand strong. With Jimmy's encouragement they were prepared to break through the police lines and forcibly prevent the Negro children from entering the school.

Violence erupted when four Negro newsmen appeared on

the scene. A shout went up, "Here come the niggers!" and the bristling crowd attacked. Twenty rednecks led the assault. They chased the newsmen back down the street, beating them, kicking them, cursing them. While the crowd was venting its fury on the newspapermen, the nine Negro children arrived in two cars and walked quietly into Central High.

Integration had been accomplished in Little Rock . . . but not for long. When the crowd realized it had been duped and the Negro children had indeed entered the school, it boiled over. It churned around Central High in a frenzy, looking for targets to smash and obliterate. There were no Negroes in sight or in reach so it turned on its next most hated enemy—the members of the Northern press. Photographers were slugged, their cameras broken. Three *Life* magazine writers were mauled and beaten. . . . And in the midst of all this bloodletting the Little Rock police acted like little more than spectators.

This freedom from police restraint encouraged the screaming mob. Now the rednecks were shrieking threats against the school; promising to tear it down, brick by brick, "if those niggers aren't kicked out." The temper of the mob was such that by noon of Little Rock's showdown day, the Mayor of the city, Woodrow Wilson Mann, ordered the nine Negro children withdrawn from Central High. . . . Mob rule had triumphed. And what did Jimmy Karam have to say to the press that day after the shouting and beatings were over? "Didn't have a thing to do with it," and he smiled charmingly, disarmingly. "I was here just watchin' out for my two kids. You know, Central High is their school."

As Jimmy Karam talks about those raucous days today, you must stretch your imagination to see him in that role. The tough edges are still there—the strong, resilient body, the pummeled face and strong jaw line—but the manner is sweet and the smile quick and easy. One might wonder how these two contradictions lived in one man.

Says Jimmy in explanation, "I think my nature—such as it was—leaned to the good side. My mother was a kind, good woman; my daddy, he was a meek, lovable man. So what was good in me, I came by naturally. The bad part . . . well, that reminds me of the old song, 'I Was a Rose in the Devil's Garden.' There was just enough of the seed of sin in me to take root. The shame and humiliation I went through because I was considered a foreigner and a Catholic did something to me. When I was old enough to think people disliked us, I decided to hate them right back. You know how it is; hate breeds hate just as love breeds love. Only in those days, I didn't know about that last part."

Following a "holiday of freedom" after his divorce, he married again. His second wife was a beautiful girl who loved him deeply and still does, he says pridefully, conceding amazement that she could stick it out so long. In those early days, he didn't trust anyone. He thought she married him for his money. The same hands-off gruffness he applied to the rest of his family—his parents, his two children, his brother and his three sisters. They loved him—all of them—for the good that was in him; but they were also afraid of him. He knew it and neither could nor would do anything to change it.

"On the one hand," he says, "I gave them all kinds of gifts and money and with the other hand I took them back again. Not the gifts, mind you, but the way I gave them; not with my love but with my spleen. There was no one in the world I could get close to because I wouldn't let them get close."

In June, 1957, Jimmy Karam went to New York with Governor Faubus. The trip was part of a campaign to promote a motion picture which extolled the virtues of the sovereign state of Arkansas. This junket was a big thing for Jimmy Karam. He had helped plan it and he looked forward to it. "The Big Town at last," he thought, "and in a big way too." Averell Harriman was New York's governor then and he had mapped out a red-carpet visit that was studded with all the creature joys the city could afford: official welcomes, police escorts, a big-league ball game and a night of it at Club "21."

Governor Faubus went along with everything but the Club "21" deal. "We're skipping that, Jimmy."

"What do you mean, skipping it? That's the best. We don't have anything like that in Little Rock. I wouldn't miss "21" for the world."

"Another time, Jimmy," the Governor said. "I have something else in mind for tonight."

"Like what?"

The Governor smiled. "Like going over to Madison Square Garden to hear Billy Graham speak."

"Billy Graham!" Jimmy Karam shouted. "Why, he's nothing but a hoot-and-hollerin' preacher. We got a million of them down home, Governor."

"But we don't have Billy Graham, Jimmy, and I want to hear Billy Graham—tonight."

And that was how Karam happened to be at Madison Square Garden during Billy Graham's New York Crusade, which lasted for sixteen weeks and saw 58,000 people respond to the evangelist's call to accept salvation. Jimmy Karam wasn't numbered among that multitude. Along with Governor Faubus, he was introduced to the Garden faithful from Billy Graham's pulpit. If nothing else, Jimmy was impressed by the turnout. Every seat in the house was taken, 18,000 of them, and there were thousands more outside who couldn't get in. Another thing that managed to seep in through Jimmy Karam's resistance was the atmosphere of the place. He had been to these revival clambakes before—just for kicks—and they were dreary affairs, all of them: the bluenose preacher, solemn and foreboding, threatening nothing but hell's fire and damnation, and the gloomy people, sitting there with their sins . . . afraid, afraid.

Here in Madison Square Garden, at the Billy Graham Crusade, the atmosphere was electric. It had the excitement and enthusiasm of a healthy political convention.

"It was as though all those people had come together to vote for God," Jimmy Karam says, "and they were happy to take their oath as citizens of heaven. Never saw anything like it." He thought for a moment. "There was something else too. It was the *variety* of people. They weren't cut all from the same cloth. They were up and down the money scale, every color in the rainbow, and every denomination you could think of."

And then there was Billy Graham himself: not a stiff-backed geezer in a frock coat and a stiff collar but a good-looking young fellow in a dark double-breasted suit, white shirt and a tie with a little splash to it. If Jimmy Karam didn't know who he was, he would have guessed the man was a successful salesman or maybe a stockbroker.

Finally, there was the message itself; strong it was, but not the raving and carrying-on like those old-time preachers who acted as though the Holy Spirit were giving them Saint Vitus's dance. The quality affected the pragmatic little campaign manager. "This guy was class. Always admired great ability. Man, I knew he had it." Along with Billy Graham's piercing voice, it was his hands that Karam remembers—those long, bony fingers of his, moving, gesticulating, emphasizing his words. . . .

Everybody is a sinner . . . everybody was born in sin . . . but everybody—anybody—can be saved. . . . How? . . . It's as simple as opening the door of your heart and letting Jesus in. . . . Simple as ABC. . . . Simple as falling off a log. . . . And how long does it take? Only a second. Only a twinkling of an eye. . . . No thinking, pondering . . . no should I or shouldn't I. . . . He's standing there, waiting for you. . . . The dearest friend, the truest love you have in this world and in eternity. . . . Open the door of your heart to Him. . . . Let Him inhabit the temple of your soul. . . . Greet Him and embrace Him as your Savior and you will escape the judgment of Almighty God and know, for sure, that heaven is your destiny. . . . All of you . . . even the blackest sinner . . . can be saved. . . . Let us pray.

Karam sat amazed as 18,000 heads bowed in prayer. After the prayer, he listened to Billy Graham invite those who wished to make decisions of repentance to enter the aisles and march to the platform. He watched the outpouring of bodies as they

walked slowly, deliberately, as though they were in the process
of transfiguration. Most of the faces were peaceful, serene. A few
broke into sobs of release.

On their way out of the Garden, Governor Faubus said,
"Well, what did you think of him, Jimmy?"

"He's got talent, all right. You can't help admiring the guy.
Never heard a preacher like him before. What were you doing,
Governor, keeping it a secret? In all the years I've known you,
you never once mentioned Billy Graham or religion or anything
like that."

The Governor smiled. "I didn't think *you'd* be interested."

He nodded. Maybe the Governor was right. All the years of
his life, before tonight, he wouldn't have been interested.

In his childhood days, going to the Catholic church was a
duty. When he became old enough not to have to, he quit, and he
never missed what he left behind. Certainly, closeness to God, in
a personal sense, never touched him. And as for the other people
who sat in the pews with him, he *knew* they didn't like him, and
he returned the compliment in kind. This new prick in his conscience was different. He suspected that here he could be accepted. The religious enthusiasm in the great hall seemed more
personal, more forgiving, and he almost felt wanted. Then the
defensiveness returned. Not so fast, he told himself. Maybe you
just got carried away by all that hoopla. Something like seeing a
good show and leaving the theater temporarily excited. The feeling that wears off after a while.

Karam returned to Little Rock, intrigued by the tableau of
Madison Square Garden. At home, Mr. Little Rock (he was given
the title by the Chamber of Commerce) didn't seem to be able
to slip easily into the usual routine. An internal nagging refused
to leave him. The familiar activities, the sweet-swinging, raucous
fun, seemed to curdle. He began asking himself, "Why?" over
and over. The answer eluded him. One answer kept insinuating
itself. He wanted to be loved, respected. But he had tackled these
prizes with football tactics, overwhelming his family and friends

with a combination of lavish generosity and unforgiveable disagreeableness while he smashed his enemies, real or apparent. His daughter, Mary Ann, noticed his discomfort.

"Daddy, what's the matter with you lately?" she asked, as they sat together in the coffee shop of a downtown department store. "You're acting so strange. All you do is sit around and mope."

"Nothing's the matter with me," he muttered, bridling with the awareness that his feelings had invaded his face.

"You sure you're all right?"

"I said I was, didn't I?"

"Business OK?" she persisted.

He slammed down his cup. "What are you bugging me for, girl? You're beginning to sound just like your mama. I'm all right, I tell you. Just leave me alone." Even as he spat out the words, he hated himself for his harshness.

"I'm sorry. I didn't mean to be a pest." She put on her gloves and started to go.

"Where you off to?"

"Off to church. Why don't you come along? You've never been to church with me. It'd make me very happy."

"Maybe you but not me. Churches and me don't go together."

"This is a *revival*. You said you went to the Billy Graham Crusade when you were in New York."

"I went because the Governor made me go." He laughed a little. "Besides, your preacher wouldn't hold a candle to Billy Graham. That fellow really puts on a show."

Mary Ann looked at him as though she didn't understand. "No preacher is 'big time,' it's God who is big time. Even Mr. Graham would tell you that. All any preacher does is work for God. You'd like Reverend Vaught. He's a good man."

Jimmy Karam lit a cigarette and drew on it impatiently. "All those preachers do is talk. . . . Most of them are hypocrites."

"I'm sorry you feel that way, Daddy."

"Don't be sorry. Just don't try to do any mumbo jumbo on me. Go on to your Baptist preacher, enjoy yourself and leave me be."

Mary Ann left without another word. Karam sat there alone, smoking and drinking coffee.

"Felt lower than a rattlesnake's belly," he says. "Didn't have to give that kid such a hard time. She's a good girl; never gave me a bit of trouble. She loves me. All she was trying to do was help. That's all everyone in my family was trying to do—love me and help me—and I bit their hands, every one of them."

For a quick moment he felt like having a drink and enjoying the easy conviviality of the "boys" around the bar. Instead, he went back to his downtown store, let the salesmen off early ("I'll close up," he told them), and then he turned off most of the lights and sat alone in his misery. He wondered about Mary Ann and whether, at that moment, she was praying or singing hymns.

Mary Ann was doing neither. She was talking with the Reverend Vaught.

"I know it's a great deal to ask of you, Reverend Vaught, but it would mean so much to me, to all of us—most of all to him."

The minister shook his head in doubt. "I don't know what to tell you, Mary Ann. I've known your father for many years and as long as I've known him, he's been anti everything, including— and especially—religion. I don't want to be unkind, but I would say he's not a very hopeful candidate for God."

"That's only because you don't know him, Mr. Vaught—really know him. He isn't all bad. Oh, I know he's behaved harshly but now I think he's beginning to know it too. He's a very unhappy man. Please talk to him."

The preacher agreed to stop by the store that night on his way home. It wasn't a happy decision and he made it reluctantly. He became more reluctant as he approached Jimmy Karam's store on his way home. He was sorry for Mary Ann but he felt unequal to his task. He reflected on the man: a troublemaker, a bully, who took pleasure from violence.

Reverend Vaught walked around the block three times before he got up enough courage to knock on the door of the dimly lighted store. When he saw Jimmy Karam emerge through the gloom, he swiftly wondered whether the man would let him in or throw him out. A betting man, he thought, would take odds on the latter. Much to the preacher's surprise, Karam waved and let him in. Karam reconstructs the conversation as follows.

"I hope I'm not bothering you, Mr. Karam," Reverend Vaught said.

Jimmy's smile was automatic, not friendly. "As long as you're here, you may as well come in."

They walked to the office, in the back of the store.

Recalling the incident, Jimmy Karam says, "I didn't like the idea of this guy barging in on me like that, so I thought I'd give him the needle."

He said, "What did you have in mind, Preacher—something in a double-breasted herringbone with two pairs of trousers and a vest thrown in?"

Reverend Vaught's distress grew. It was clear that if Karam wasn't going to throw him out of the store, he was going to sneer him out. He remembered his promise to Mary Ann and steeled himself against the worst.

"What I had in mind, Mr. Karam, was not clothing but *you*. I thought perhaps I could help you in a way that money and material success alone has failed you. I thought, maybe, I could offer *you* some clothing—a mantle of peace and love that you could wear proudly for all the world to see."

Jimmy Karam thought that was pretty smart talking. He hadn't thought the preacher had it in him—took his own words and threw them right back at him.

He laughed. "That sounds like a nice piece of goods, Pastor, but I doubt that it would fit me. Even if it did, it might not be my style."

"It's everybody's style, Mr. Karam. It's everybody's measurements. All you have to do is try it on for size."

The device of mock banter lightened the air between them.

"OK, Mr. Vaught. Drag out your samples and let me see what you have to offer."

The preacher offered peace on earth through love of God and everlasting life beyond. The lofty expansiveness, the confident conviction of the preacher's message was nevertheless stated simply, utterly devoid of pulpiteering histrionics.

Jimmy Karam shrugged. "You do a good sales pitch, Mr. Vaught, but what's the price? What do I have to pay for all this glory hallelujah?"

"Nothing, Mr. Karam—not a red cent. All you have to do is find your way to God through Jesus Christ. No taxes, no tolls; just the assurance that you need God just as God *needs you, wants you, loves you.*"

Jimmy Karam listened and didn't speak. Then the minister stopped talking. For a moment the silence between them grew embarrassingly turgid.

"I hope you'll forgive me for coming here this way, Mr. Karam. You were very patient to listen."

"I listen to anybody, Mr. Vaught. Can't say that I buy everything they try to sell, but I listen. . . . It don't hurt to listen."

Relieved that he had made even this progress, the minister put on his hat, said good night and left.

Jimmy Karam sat in his darkened shop a long time that night. Hours after the pastor had left, he kept hearing his words: "God needs you, wants you, loves you." That was what Billy Graham had said back there in Madison Square Garden during his New York Crusade. . . . "But what does God want *me* for?" he asked himself. "After all *I've* been, after all *I've* done. . . ."

When he came home that night he found his wife waiting up for him. "You all right, Jimmy?" Her voice was shaded with concern.

"Sure, I'm all right. What's going on here?"

"Mary Ann told me that Mr. Vaught was going to be in the store tonight—"

He interrupted her. "And you were worried because you thought I might throw him out on his duff. Right?"

"Well, I know how upset you get when anyone talks religion to you. I know how you feel about those things, Jimmy."

Jimmy Karam shook his head. "If you do, it's more than I know, because I don't know how I feel any more . . . for sure."

She looked at him, wondering what he meant, but afraid even to ask.

"Something's happening to me, honey. I don't know what it is, but whatever it is, it keeps growing, getting bigger and bigger —and I keep getting smaller and smaller."

He stopped and smiled at the look of puzzlement on his wife's face.

"I guess you know something happened to me in New York when I heard Billy Graham speak, don't you? I didn't want to go. I got so mad at the Governor for dragging me along, I could have packed up and left, then and there. But I stayed and it began to happen. Until then the world was my oyster, but this Graham guy was dropping a grain of irritating sand into it. And that's how pearls are born, honey. That's how pearls are *born!*"

"What are you talking about, Jimmy?"

"This thing that's *in* me. That's what I'm talking about." He heard himself almost shouting, so he stopped.

She moved over to him, took his hand and held it. "You've made up your mind about something, Jimmy. Tell me what it is."

"I want to be baptized, honey. I want to be a real Christian more than anything in the world—and I want it now or as soon as it's humanly possible."

His wife began to cry, that special way happy women cry. "Oh, Jimmy, I'm so glad. Let's be baptized together."

They would have called Pastor Vaught that night if it hadn't been so late. When they did call him in the morning, it was too late for that day. Mr. Vaught had gone to Tuscaloosa and wouldn't be back until the end of the week. It was a great disappointment for Jimmy Karam.

"Maybe it's God's will, Jimmy," his wife said. "Maybe he's

testing us to see if what we want now we'll still want two days from now."

Karam remembers vividly the night of their baptism.

"It was a Saturday night," he says, "and somehow the word got around about what was going to happen. Folks just wouldn't believe it. 'Oh, no,' they said, 'not Jimmy Karam, not that rough-house head, that troublemaker. Him baptized? Him a Christian? It'd be enough to make a saint turn over in his grave.' They just wouldn't believe it," he says, "and because they wouldn't believe it, they came out in droves to see it happen. One newspaper guy later said it was the greatest baptism since Saint Paul of Tarsus. He knew me, he thought, and he still wouldn't believe it."

And after it happened . . . what happened to Jimmy Karam?

Jimmy Karam thinks a minute before he answers. Then, when he speaks, he leaves no doubt about his convictions.

"I suppose I divide my witness to Christ into two parts. The first is how it affects me, and the second, how it affects the people around me. Personally, I never felt so good. It's like Billy Graham and Pastor Vaught say. I was born again, all over again, and when I opened my eyes, I saw things I never really saw before—all of God's work: the sky, the trees, a leaf, a bird, the color of air, the good smell of morning."

Jimmy Karam paused as though he were looking for words that would be equal to his thoughts. "When I think of it now, it's as though I spent all of my life—until my conversion—halfway under ether, seeing nothing, feeling nothing, knowing nothing. . . . It's the opposite of what the Communists say. They tell you that religion is the opiate of the masses. Not true. It's the other way around. Sin is the opiate—smoking, drinking, gambling, womanchasing. Those are the things that dull the senses, that pull the shades over your eyes.

"Sure, I gave up all of them. From two packs of cigarettes a day I went to two packs of nothing a day. I tested myself and it worked. Stopped dead, just like that. Never missed them. Never wanted them any more. That went for drinking, gambling, everything. It was like opening up a window in a foul dungeon. The good clean air rushes in and dilutes the offenders until they're washed out."

And what about the other part of Jimmy Karam's witness— the part that affected the people around him?

"That's easy," he says. "You take my family. Never believed they loved me for me alone. Thought my wife married me for my money. Thought my kids and my brother and sisters loved me only for what I could give them. Never trusted any of them. Never believed them. I went my way and they went theirs; even my wife and I. We had nothing in common. Now it's different. We all love Christ together. We all have Him in our hearts.

"Just to show you," he went on, "what's happened to me and my wife: Used to spend as little time as possible home. Left in the morning—if I was home at all that night—and came back late enough to find her sleeping. Now I'm home every night, have dinner with the family and, when it's time for bed, we take out the Bible. I read a verse to my wife and then she reads one to me. And we thank God for what has happened to us."

Then Jimmy Karam goes on to tell how his conversion to Christ affected the people of Little Rock.

"Let's start with Governor Faubus," he says. "The whole world blamed him for all the violence in Little Rock. Not so. What I did, I did. Half the time I kept him from knowing what was really going on. The other half I carried out his bidding—but in my own way. And my own way was violence. Without a roughneck like me at his fingertips there wouldn't have been anything near the trouble we had in Little Rock. . . . Tell you something funny, but it proves my point: When Governor Faubus heard about my conversion to Christ, he called me in. He told me he was happy for me. He wished me luck in my new life. I'm out of politics. We're still very good friends."

And the ordinary citizens of Little Rock—both the whites and the Negroes—how did Jimmy Karam's conversion to Christ change their lives?

"The same way that it changed my life," he answers. "You

can set an example, and it's either a good example or a bad one. Now I was setting a good example. I helped set up an organization called We Who Care, and we who cared dedicated ourselves to doing good instead of doing bad. I told angry, bitter people how much easier it was to love instead of hate; how much easier it was to use your energy for good instead of harm. And, most of all, how much better off *they* would be. I told them that Christianity wasn't talking, it was *doing*."

Jimmy Karam said it over and over again to any and all who would listen. He spoke at business meetings, youth and church groups and club luncheons. No one had to ask him twice to deliver his message of tolerance and love. And if they were reluctant to ask him, he would ask them. The people who heard him were impressed. They knew what Jimmy Karam had been and they knew what he was now.

"The change didn't come overnight," he insists. "The moral condition of a city isn't much different from its physical condition. If a city's dirty, you have to clean it up street by street, neighborhood by neighborhood. I told them I wasn't asking them to *give* the Negroes something. I was demanding that they return the rights we had stolen from them."

It worked. Little by little the hard crust of hate and intolerance crumbled. Little by little the crusade for decency and law seeped into the private homes and the public places of Little Rock until a far step toward integration became an accepted fact; in the schools, the movie houses, the hotels, the restaurants, wherever people had the right to be together.

"Don't let anyone tell you that we are doing any favors for the Negro. He owns his rights no less than anyone else. The debt is too long overdue."

These are Jimmy Karam's words and if there are any who doubt the sincerity of them, they should have seen him during the period of the riots in Cambridge, Maryland, and, in Birmingham, the bombings that snuffed out the lives of children, and the attacks by police dogs on civil rights marchers. The ex-tough fought back the tears. "I've always been sorry that I didn't go there and let them sic the dogs on me, too. Would have taught a lot of people a lesson," he says.

"It's got to stop," he continues. "Those people have to see God's will through Jesus Christ. It's the only way to stop all this hating, all this violence. Love is the only answer. People have to love everyone—black as well as white. It's the only answer. I can't say it enough."

Karam is obsessed with the desire to say it. He spends most of his days away from his successful clothing stores. He travels up and down the state, proclaiming his own personal convictions, not only in words but in deeds.

In 1963, for example, Karam, who was then the elected Commander of an American Legion post in Little Rock, went out on a shaky limb. He issued an order banning liquor and gambling in his Legion post. The result was a hoot-and-hollering bedlam meeting during which calls for his impeachment were loud and long. But Jimmy stood his ground. Drinking and gambling were, in his view, wrong. Each individual had the right to do as he wished. But officially, the Legion should not be in the business of aiding and abetting the practices. Karam won out. Even his hard-drinking detractors and compulsive gamblers had to admit that, in principle, he was right.

"God has made a place for me," he says, "just as He can make a place for everyone who opens his heart. . . . I always wanted to be as good a man as I hope I am now. I didn't have the strength. I lied, I cheated, I gambled, I fought and I caroused. The devil was in me and I couldn't fight him because I couldn't replace him. Once I accepted Jesus Christ as my Savior, my devil died."

And if someone says "Amen" to that, Jimmy Karam smiles and takes his hand.

"Amen," he repeats. "So be it for all men."

ELEANOR
SEARLE WHITNEY

The Mission of a Socialite

"WITHOUT MY faith I would have been a candidate for the bottle, the needle or the psychiatrist's couch."

The speaker is a woman who bears little resemblance to those foreboding words. She is tall, strikingly attractive, impeccably groomed. Her audience is a group of five hundred professional and business women, smiling and nodding as she speaks.

"Eight years ago," Eleanor Whitney tells them, "I *called* myself a Christian. I had been reared in a Christian home, had been baptized in infancy and later confirmed. But at my confirmation I was conscious only that I was being accepted as a member of the church. I had not yet been confronted by Jesus Christ. To me, He was a rather vague being who had given His name to a religion into which I had the good fortune to be born. My church membership was very little different from a club membership. I had no personal relationship with God. And you see, ladies, being a true Christian (not just a church member) is a personal way of life. It's something no one can teach you or do for you. Each of us has to do it for herself. It's true that Christians can be organized, but joining an organization does not make one a Christian. It is a personal decision."

Eleanor Whitney spoke to the ladies for more than an hour, stopping now and then to sing a hymn that emphasized her words.

Singing is a very integral part of her message. She opens and closes her talk with song. Her trained voice rings true; every syllable of the lyrics reaches the far corners of the banquet room.

After the meeting was over, dozens filed to the speaker's table to shake her hand, thank her for joining them and tell her that her appearance was responsible for one of the largest turnouts in the organization's history.

"I'm sure it's true. It was a good turnout," she said later on over a cup of tea. "But I know that a lot of those dear ladies came to the meeting tonight because I'm Eleanor Whitney, because eight years ago I was all over the front pages with my sensational divorce case, because I've made the lists of the Ten Best Dressed and I was the first recipient of the Golden Hat Award from the American Millinery Institute. I wear colorful clothes because they match my personality and they match my religion. True Christianity *is* colorful. It's rich, vibrant and up to date. It never goes out of style."

It does not trouble her that some of the women came to the meeting to satisfy their curiosity about a sensational glamour woman.

"I don't mind at all. Thousands of people come to hear Johnny Spence because he was a great golfer who led a notorious existence. Thousands more come to hear Jimmy Karam because he was Governor Faubus' bully boy. None of us worry as to why they come. All we care about is that they do come."

After the waitress served the second cup of tea, Eleanor Whitney took her hand. "Read any good books lately?" she asked.

The waitress flushed and remained silent.

"Here, try this. It's one of the best," she said to the girl, taking from her large handbag a little booklet called "Becoming a Christian," by J. R. W. Stott, chaplain to Elizabeth, Queen of England.

The flustered waitress thanked her, looked at the title and scurried away.

Eleanor Whitney smiled. "She thinks I'm some kind of religious nut. But if she reads it, it will open her eyes and maybe her heart."

The contrast of the lady of the Blue Book peddling Scripture in a coffee shop inspires curiosity concerning the journey from one road to the next. A tentative question involves the public heartbreak of her divorce.

"No, not my divorce. That's what everyone thinks, first off. It's the obvious conclusion but not the right one. A lot of people have turned to Christ out of external misery. But just as many— the ones you don't hear about—do so because they simply feel personal needs for spiritual dependence."

Then she discusses the thousands of successful, normal men and women she has seen and talked to in the past eight years on lecture platforms, in churches, at White House prayer meetings, even in the deep fastness of Africa.

"I can tell you, their encounter with God's love has been an eye-opener for me too." The woman who received notoriety for her $3 million divorce settlement from Cornelius Vanderbilt Whitney sighs. "My only regret is that I didn't see the light earlier in my life. It would have saved me a lot of childhood fears and foolish fancies."

Earlier in her life Eleanor Whitney was the small-town girl who never dreamed of the future that lay ahead of her. How could she? Plymouth, Ohio (population 2,000), had no reputation as the birthplace of the famous or the wealthy. It was a typical Midwest hamlet; pleasant enough for the old and the young but offering little to the growing teen-ager.

"That didn't bother me very much," she remembers. "I loved our little town and I dearly loved my father and mother. Daddy was a doctor, also the major public-health official of the town. He was an Anglican, born in London. Mother was a native, a fourth-generation Lutheran, whose grandfather had founded and built the Lutheran Church in our community. I was a sickly child with a chronic heart condition. I was always in mortal fear of dying and every time I had an attack, I thought it was the end for me."

Because of her handicap, which restricted her physical activities, she busied herself in those areas which called for cerebral stamina—social work and projects educational and cultural. But more important than these outside interests was the help she could give to her father. Frequently she helped him in the operating or delivery room when a leg had to be amputated, an appendix removed or a baby brought into the world.

"You know, whenever I go home to Plymouth now people invariably trot out the once-upon-a-time children I helped Daddy deliver or those I helped Daddy divorce from their tonsils. It's a real joy to see them all again.

"In my church work I was a whirling dervish. Aside from attending church regularly, I was up to my ears in Sunday school, Bible classes, church suppers—but most of all in singing. On many a weekend, I would be the soloist for five services. Oh, there was no doubt in my mind that I was the living, breathing essence of Christianity."

That comfort prevailed until a pair of college friends, home for the holidays, asked Eleanor if she was a Christian. The question not only bewildered her, it annoyed her.

"Are you serious?" she asked them, while reciting her devotion to the church, capping it all with the declaration that she was not only a Christian but a confirmed one.

Confirmed to what, they wanted to know.

"That really threw me," she laughs, remembering her confusion at the time. "I realized that, to me, confirmation meant little more than a word, a ritual. But those college kids set me straight."

"Confirmation, Eleanor, means that you confirm your acceptance of Jesus as God in the flesh, and that you acknowledge Him as your Savior, take Him as your Lord and Master, the only one who can save you from the consequences of your own sins."

She shakes her head, shrugs her elegant stole-clad shoulders. "I thought that was very neat but just a little too-too . . . if you know what I mean. Besides, I had heard something of the same kind of 'pitch' from my mother, who was the only real 'born-again Christian' I had ever known. And while I loved her dearly, I thought her concept of religion was, to use the vernacular, s-q-u-a-r-e. So I went on my merry way, secure in my belief that I was as good a Christian as anyone else, if not better."

It would be difficult to find a handful of people in Plymouth, Ohio, who didn't agree with young Eleanor. She *was* a good Christian; better than most. Not only did she conform to the general precepts of her faith, she extended herself to make them a reality. As she grew into her late teens, her ambitions took shape. Music became her serious choice.

"But how can you be serious about music in a town the size of Plymouth? Naturally, I had to go where music was created and performed and written about. New York, where else? Don't get the idea that I set the world on fire when I hit the big town. New York is a wonderful city but it's like trial by fire: fierce competition, blazing ambitions, all-consuming vanities. It's no place for the fainthearted, I can tell you."

The size and pace of the metropolis left her stimulated and dizzy. "You won't believe it, Daddy," she wrote to her father, "but there are more people in some apartment houses here than we have in all of Plymouth! It's frightening in a way but it's also fun and exhilarating."

She had inherited the sense of adventure from her great-grandfather who had struck out from the civilized East in 1832 to try his fortunes in the little-known and rugged Midwest. From her mother's grandfather, Felix Fenner, she inherited musical genes; he had been an accomplished church organist.

She wasn't really alone in the big city, because arrangements had been made for her to live with Mme. Ella Toedt, who was to serve as her combined vocal teacher, landlady and school adviser. Between them they decided on Columbia University, where Eleanor took courses in the humanities: art, music, languages. Mme. Toedt was also helpful in placing Eleanor as a soloist in a Lutheran church and in a synagogue.

"Singing in a synagogue was a wonderful experience," she says. "I enjoyed every minute of it for five years. I didn't know

Hebrew then. I sang phonetically. The words were spelled out in English syllables. Later on, of course, I did learn to read the language. And let me tell you something, buster, I have one of the best Hebrew accents this side of Tel Aviv. But aside from the joy of singing in a synagogue, it was such a wonderful experience to be with the Jews. These were the seeds of Abraham, the chosen ones of God, the members of the family of Jesus. I felt so close to them and, half the time, I envied them."

When Eleanor Whitney turned twenty, she decided to strive for an operatic goal, despite the strenuous physical demands it would impose on her. Her father, familiar with her chronic heart condition, advised against it. "Don't worry, Daddy," she wrote him, "I'll go as far as I can without killing myself."

Her career took her through performances on the concert stage with the Saint Louis Municipal Opera Company in *The Fire-fly, Katinka, Rose Marie* and other productions, as a radio artist with the National Broadcasting Company and a touring member of the Madrigal Singers.

"Daddy was right," she admits now. "I just didn't have the stamina for grand opera." Then she stops and laughs. "Oh, but you're not interested in a once-upon-a-time singing career. What you really want to hear about is my marriage to Sonny Whitney and all the gory details that went with it. Right? Everyone wants to hear about it. It's my claim to fame. And let's not be overly tactful about it. I don't mind any more. There was a time when I did, when I got the absolute horrors just remembering it. But that's all over and done with now. Thanks to my new faith I've learned to live a new life. I don't live in the past—only the future. Sonny and I were married for eighteen years. But it wasn't the length of the marriage. It was the people—him and me."

"Sonny," of course, is Cornelius Vanderbilt Whitney, the millionaire sportsman, socialite, industrialist.

Eleanor Whitney shakes her head. "Not 'millionaire,' dearie —*multi*millionaire."

Whitney's ancestor, Isaiah Whitney, emigrated to the States from England in the 1760s. His grandfather, William C. Whitney, founded the family fortune, and was Secretary of the Navy in President Cleveland's cabinet. His father, Henry Payne Whitney, was the world-famous sportsman, who left a fortune estimated at $50 million. His mother, the heiress daughter of the Vanderbilts, was a prominent dowager-sculptress. Sonny was reared with the trappings familiar to those to the manner born. After his graduation from Yale, where he was a varsity crewman, he enjoyed fame as an all-round outdoor sportsman, mining tycoon, chairman of the board of Pan American Airways, owner of the fabulous Whitney stable of race horses, director of the Metropolitan Opera Company and the American Museum of Natural History. In World War II he served diligently as a flying instructor in the Army Air Corps.

"That was the Sonny Whitney the world knew, that *I* knew when I first met him," his divorced wife tells you. She hesitates and smiles. "You know, very few people really know how I met Sonny. The general impression—and that goes for the newspaper people too—is that we met through our mutual musical interests; either socially or professionally. After all, he was a patron of the opera and I was a singer. Figures, doesn't it? Not so. Actually, we met in a most peculiar way."

The "most peculiar way" fell into the coziest tradition of a storybook romance. It took place during a hot New York summer, when performing artists hibernate, awaiting fall and the renewal of the theatrical season. Eleanor's roommate, who worked as a receptionist in the offices of Pan American Airways, was due for a vacation and suggested that Eleanor fill in for her.

"It was honest, simple work and I didn't see any reason why I shouldn't take it. Besides, in the off-season, I could use the money and the job wouldn't interfere with my church and synagogue singing. I was something of a freak at Pan Am. The reception desk had never played host to a professional singer, and everyone thought it was 'very interesting,' including Sonny."

He would stop at the desk and chat about her career. Later on, he would call her into his office, where they could discuss music and opera at greater length. When her roommate returned from vacation and resumed her job, Whitney called the unemployed singer at her apartment.

"I'd be less than truthful if I didn't say I was hoping he would. On the other hand, I was a little afraid and awed by him; not only because of his wealth and position. His reputation with the ladies bothered me not a little. You see, Sonny was divorced from his first wife, legally separated from his second, and—as they say in sporting circles—playing the field to keep in practice."

Eleanor Whitney laughs. "I really had qualms. I had no desire to be a passing filly in the great sportsman's life. I was too much in love with him."

Her roommate offered some no-nonsense advice. "How can you be so naïve! I don't know a girl who wouldn't give her right arm to have a date with Cornelius Vanderbilt Whitney! And you sit there playing the 'should I or shouldn't I' game. Come off it. You're a big girl. You know how to say no if you want to."

Much to her surprise, Eleanor was never tested. Sonny Whitney announced that he loved her and asked to marry her.

"Believe it or not, I was still nervous," she says. "I didn't want to be number three in a long string of wives, à la Tommy Manville."

"That's up to you, Eleanor," her roommate told her. "You have to see to it that you're the last wife he'll ever have. It could be a man-size job with a man like Mr. Whitney, but if anyone can do it, you can. You've got everything going for you."

Eleanor's next offering of moral support came from Sonny Whitney's mother. "He needs you, Eleanor. If you love him, I think you can make him the wife he always wanted. I don't know how you feel about having me as a mother-in-law, but I like the idea of having you as my daughter-in-law."

The wedding took place in Plymouth, Ohio, in the First Lutheran Church, founded by Felix Fenner, Eleanor's great-grandfather.

For the ceremony, Whitney transported his private photographer and press agent and a flood of his favorite vintage champagne. "It was quite a splashy affair," Mrs. Whitney recalls with a chuckle. "It had all the trappings of a royal wedding. And in Plymouth, Ohio! Sonny had a flair for the extravaganza."

They began their married life in the same extravaganza tradition of the landed gentry, light-years removed from Plymouth, Ohio.

"It was simply incredible," she says. "Especially for a recent hick like me. We had everything: houses here and abroad, apartments in our favorite cities, fishing camps, stables, cars, yachts, airplanes, clothes, furs, jewels, servants and money, money, money. You name it, we had it. And if we didn't have it, Sonny could buy it—by the carload."

However, despite the material blessings she enjoyed, there were disappointments and frustrations that money could neither prevent nor erase. Although Sonny's first two marriages had produced three offspring, her own marriage—for a long time—was barren. Her less than robust physical condition brought on a succession of miscarriages. When her one living child was born, he wasn't expected to live. Somehow, after fearsome crises, he overcame his initial deficiencies and survived.

Then there was Sonny Whitney himself. . . .

"There was this restlessness in him," she says in measured words that reflect a long struggle to understand him. "Many men have it. Some of them try to pacify it with drink, others with gambling, hobbies, accumulating money or what have you. With Sonny, it was the ladies. And I have reason to suspect they were more than occasional. The chase—and conquest—must have proved something to him. Before my marriage, it was the thing I was most afraid of. I believed in marriage, the whole bit; a vow is a vow—'Till death do you part'—and I still do. So I hung on, swallowing each hurt silently. At first, when he would disappear for days or for weeks, I would say it was my fault. I didn't have what it took to hold him, I told myself. Then I remembered his two ex-wives. Didn't they have it either? And what about my suspected rivals? Their staying power couldn't have been anything to write home about because, sooner or later, he came back."

Despite the pain, she resolved to encourage none of the typical husband-and-wife postmortems characteristic of such situations—the accusations, threats, tears and recriminations.

"I had a different approach," she explains. "I figured he had gone through all that before. I said nothing. I acted as though he hadn't even been away; as though I didn't even suspect or dream what he had been doing. And if he was contrite or offered apologies or attempted to promise it would never happen again, I would shush him before he could say two words.

"I played for time, plain, old rotten time, hoping that he would get tired of it all; that one day he would wake up realizing it was good to be home and find the whole chasing business a big bore. . . . Of course, it didn't work, but for eighteen long years I tried. And when it was over, it was over for him but not for me. In retrospect I can't say the years were very good, but they were not really bad either, because I wouldn't let them be bad. By nature I'm a happy and optimistic kook. If today is a bad day for me, I always feel that tomorrow is bound to be better. So I put up a good front and went about the business of living: running our big house out in Old Westbury, Long Island, taking an active part in community, social and church life, and tending to my charity causes. Then there were the visits from Sonny's children by his former marriages. The kids enjoyed coming to the house and I enjoyed having them. Gail Whitney—she was the youngest of his three, by his second marriage—eventually came to live with us. She was a sickly girl in her late teens. Leukemia—a dreadful disease."

With compassion, Mrs. Whitney reveals another facet of her former husband's personality. He didn't entirely enjoy having his daughter living with them. It wasn't that he didn't love her; he shrank from an atmosphere of sickness. Mrs. Whitney's friends freely reveal what she is reluctant to discuss—the details of how she nursed and cared for her husband's daughter until the end of her very young life. When the girl died, her stepmother sobbed at the bedside. Sonny Whitney was away.

"To nonreligious people, death is a terrible thing. It's the end, the nothingness, the no-more," Eleanor explains. "Sonny was like that. Most people are. I know better; death is a bridge between this life and the everlasting one that can be everyone's if he would open his heart to God and believe."

She recalls her own tremors as a sickly girl in Plymouth when the specter of death confronted her.

"In those days I was only a *nominal* Christian," she explains. "Today I'm a *reborn* Christian and only eight years old by Christ's own calendar. . . . Oh, you don't know how wonderful it is not to fear death any more; not really to fear anything."

She discusses her mother—well advanced in age now—who recently underwent surgery for the amputation of a leg because of a circulatory disorder. The elderly Mrs. Searle took her daughter's hand and looked into her worried face as they prepared to wheel her into the operating room.

"Now, don't you fret, darling," she said. "It doesn't matter whether I go home to be with my Father while I'm on the operating table or a year from now. I know where I'm going to spend eternity."

"Ten years before, I wouldn't have understood her. Our faith helped both of us through that terrible ordeal."

It was faith too that helped her through the agony of her broken marriage.

"I don't know what I would have done without it. I don't know where I'd be now. But let me tell you something, dear," she says, shaking a finger in mock admonition, "don't *you* jump to the conclusion—the way 'most everyone does—that I turned to Christ *because* of my divorce. Not that it matters why or when one turns to faith; any reason or any time is a combination of the best that can ever happen to anyone. It's just a matter of setting the record straight."

The worsening state of her marriage, coinciding with the oncoming events of Billy Graham's first crusade in New York, culminated in the resolution of Eleanor Whitney's life.

"The events that led to my conversion are practically a social commentary as well as a religious revelation," she says.

To her circle of friends at Old Westbury—socialites, financiers, the horsey set—religion and Christianity were a kind of grudging duty for all.

"Of course, we attended church regularly, but for our kind of people, attending church was something like attending the annual horse or flower show or the Cotillion Ball. We dressed to the hilt and showed ourselves off to one another. Churchgoing was just an excuse for getting together and having a sumptuous brunch afterward. Naturally, we all belonged to the Episcopalian church. It was the most fashionable and the most 'civilized,' if you know what I mean: just the right amount of ritual without any embarrassing 'Bible beating.' "

It was at one of these after-church brunches that Eleanor Whitney found herself drafted as an unenthusiastic hostess to Billy Graham. Her Episcopalian rector had asked her if she would mind having Dr. Graham and his team of crusaders join them.

"I agreed reluctantly," she admits. "I didn't think that I, or any of my friends, would relish contact with a flashy Carolina preacher who had come to save us. On the other hand, I thought it couldn't do much harm. It might turn out to be the 'conversation piece' of the day."

Billy Graham arrived with his wife and his "team"—eight gentlemen who looked like eight business executives attending a sales conference. She recalls that she had an absolutely neutral reaction to all of them. "When our rector asked Billy to say a few words, I said to myself, 'Oh, God, here's where the man really does me in.' I expected a real old-fashioned revival performance —you know, the shouting and the carrying on and the Bible beating. 'Hardly an Episcopalian's dish of tea,' I thought. 'It'll take me years to live this down.' "

To her astonishment Graham talked simply and persuasively.

"The greatest stumbling block to the kingdom of Christ is pride—ego," he said. "The 'I' has to be crucified, the ego denied. No one knows better than I that some people who come forward to accept Christ at my meetings are not sincere. Their so-called conversion is a fleeting thing, a motion or an emotion in God's direction. But for those—and now I speak of the majority of people who come forward—for those who give their hearts, their minds and their souls to Christ in one unstinting gift of humility, they experience a transformation—a sweeping, wonderful, radical change that gives their lives a whole new direction. They are born again."

Eleanor Whitney looked at her friends—among them the Archibald Roosevelts, Mrs. Thomas Hitchcock, the Howard Brokaws, Count and Countess Eugene de Rothschild and Supreme Court Justice and Mrs. Stanley Reed—and saw none smile or sneer.

"We were all impressed. Suddenly it was as though something deep inside us had stirred a little. Oh, I don't mean that any of us took the plunge. After all, we were modern, *civilized* Christians. That 'old-time religion' was for old-fashioned people. But, as I say, we were impressed—enough so that we put together a car caravan that week and dozens of us drove to Madison Square Garden to attend the Billy Graham Crusade."

Eleanor Whitney admits that the attitude of the Old Westbury crowd was hardly that of a religious pilgrimage. Rather, it was a titillating curiosity to see and hear the renowned preacher in his own bailiwick. The girls were impressed enough by the overflow crowd that filled every seat of the huge Garden and spilled out into the streets.

"I was little more than a spectator; a very interested spectator but no more than that, really. I listened to the mass hymn singing, then the solo gospel singing, the introductory remarks by one of Billy's team, more singing and, finally, Billy himself. I recognized that he was a gifted pulpiteer. Later, they came forward to be saved in droves. I thought it was fine for them because *they* needed it. But not for me. I was on good terms with God. I didn't have to make a public display to prove it."

Eleanor Whitney's reactions were similar to those of her

friends who had been with her that night. While they readily agreed that Graham was a positive force for good and for God, they cringed at the exhibitionistic idea of walking down the aisle, past thousands of pairs of eyes. One of them said it was like bathing in public. They did, however, universally agree that Graham's appeal was ecumenical rather than parochial. They thought it enlightening to see counselors of every denomination at work, so that a Baptist convert could be guided by a Baptist counselor, Methodists by a Methodist counselor, and so on.

"All of us wanted to go again sometime but we were prodded into activity by two factors: one was our rector, who encouraged us to go as often as we could, and the other was the scores of telephone calls we received from people on the Island who wanted to go along with us on our next caravan to Madison Square Garden. Overnight, I found myself a celebrity, more for my religious activity than for my social ones. . . . In a way, it was an anomalous position for me. I certainly wasn't a Billy Graham convert. But many believed otherwise, since I had welcomed his team to my house and helped organize the car caravan."

Throughout the crusade, undercurrents of disapproval swirled within the starchy confines of the community. The ladies were tagged the "Cadillac Christians." Parishioners of the conservative churches grumbled that the Billy Graham "binge" was a fad that wouldn't last the summer and, by fall, the ladies would probably switch to Zen Buddhism and, by winter, return to the bosom of the pure Episcopal Church, which they shouldn't have left in the first place.

At subsequent visits to the Garden, Eleanor Whitney began to feel a pressing urge to stand up, walk down the aisle and make her own decision.

"Of course, I didn't. I rationalized my reluctance in a dozen different ways: I already was a Christian. I thought religion was a private affair. I didn't want to make a spectacle of myself and become the laughingstock of Old Westbury."

Yet the urge intensified. Even when she was home alone, it

was difficult for her to deny it. She remembered Graham's words about destroying the ego and crucifying the "I" in your life. And she remembered something else—the story of Nicodemus as told in John 3: 1–8. Nicodemus had always been her favorite Biblical character. There he was, a devout Jew, a Pharisee, the strictest of all the Jewish sects. Nicodemus prayed two hours a day, fasted two days a week, tithed, and went to the synagogue seven times a day. He was a member of the Sanhedrin—the supreme council and tribunal of the Jews—and his knowledge of religion and God's laws was unsurpassed. Yet this man Nicodemus, this most pious of men, felt a wanting in his soul. So he came to Jesus in the dark of night—he, too, didn't want to be seen and reviled—and asked why he was uneasy in his life and how he could be sure that Jesus was his redeemer. And Jesus said there was only one way for this holy man to satisfy his doubts. Nicodemus must accept Christ as his Messiah, the expected king and deliverer of the Hebrews. And when Nicodemus made his decision, erased his ego and accepted Christ into his heart, his life took on a meaning he had never known before.

Eleanor Whitney sighs when she relates the story. "I was like Nicodemus. Just as he was a good Jew, I was a good Christian—but not good enough. Like Nicodemus, I too had to accept Christ in the flesh and blood. . . . It wasn't easy for me. I too had to come in the dead of night. After the first flurry of enthusiasm for the car caravan to Madison Square Garden had worn off, I drove to Madison Square Garden alone. And there, with all my friends safely tucked away in Old Westbury, I followed Graham's urging and committed murder on my ego. I crucified the 'I' in my life and went forward.

"With me, it was just as it was with Nicodemus. I was enveloped and flooded with light. It was as though I were walking out of a dark, clammy life that held no promise for me except death and taxes, into the everlasting warmth of God's heaven, where I would live forever. . . . I cried as I walked down the aisle to the platform where Billy Graham and his counselors stood waiting for me, but my tears were tears of joy and relief. At that moment, I wouldn't have cared if the whole township of Old Westbury was watching."

Eleanor later discovered that she was not alone, among her co-caravaners, in her commitment. Several of her good friends and neighbors in Old Westbury had made the Madison Square Garden pilgrimage just as she did, alone and in the dark of night, and, like Eleanor and Nicodemus, had also walked forward.

"Wasn't that extraordinary?" she asks, her brown eyes sparkling with the wonder of it. "Each of us found our way to God separately as we were finding our way together."

Somehow, as one looks at her, sitting there, smiling with genuine happiness, one is reminded of a newspaper story about her that appeared in a Midwest journal. "Eleanor Searle Whitney," it read, "is like a child who wanders along the beach and finds a precious shell. . . . She runs back to the others imploring, 'Come, give me your hand and I will take you to the place where I found my treasure! It is for everyone. You too can find it.' "

The description is particularly apt because she exudes an aura of youthful, feminine honesty untrammeled by maturity and sophistication. The quality achieves a new silhouette when the cruel hurts of her marriage failure and its tabloid notoriety are recalled.

"It wasn't easy," she admits. "I loved my husband. I still regard him as one of the finest men I've ever known."

The humiliation of public desertion inflicted wounds of a depth only a woman in such a plight could understand. A "small" incident involving a diamond brooch, a Christmas present he had given her just before the final break in their marriage, stimulates a tone of sad reminiscence. "It was a beautiful brooch, a wonderful Christmas gift. I adored it. . . . Yes, he took it back and gave it to the girl who was to become his fourth wife. I happened to run into them at the opera one night and she was wearing it." She laughs, throwing the incident over her shoulder. "I must say it looked lovely on her. Sonny wasn't just saving money on a gift. I guess the brooch had a particular meaning for him. It had been intended as a gift of love but his love had been transferred from me to someone else, so the gift had to go along with the transference. I'm really not trying to be magnanimous. Just trying to understand. Sonny is not a villain. He's a very complicated man and while a complicated man is capable of a villainous deed, it doesn't necessarily follow that villainy is an essential part of a complicated man."

She applies the thesis to the unsavory airing of the Whitney separation and divorce.

"Our society is so constituted that wherever there is conflict there has to be a villain. And who is more adept at creating villains than lawyers and newspapermen? You see, poor Sonny had the cards stacked against him. I was his third wife. He was a three-time loser, as the saying goes. Besides, he was a Whitney scion who had inherited $50 million. It was a little difficult for anyone to be in that heavyweight's corner."

She fought him—both in and out of court. "Out of court because I really loved him and wanted to hold on to him; because our son needed a father just as much as he needed me. And I fought him in court despite that good old Christian precept of turning the other cheek. The trouble with turning the other cheek with a man like Sonny," she explains, "is that after seventeen years your cheeks are worn to a frazzle. Besides, there's another Christian precept, which says that man must pay for the hurt he inflicts upon others. My first legal action was to file a suit for separation. This was to prevent Sonny from obtaining a divorce. I wasn't after a quickie divorce and a fat alimony check."

Whitney had asked for a divorce, suggesting that she get it in Las Vegas. In exchange he offered her a very generous settlement. When she refused, he flew to Las Vegas himself.

To block the divorce, she countered by filing suit for legal separation, requesting neither temporary alimony nor even counsel fees. In a prepared statement, Whitney said: "I am both shocked and amazed by Mrs. Whitney's action. Ever since she rejected a very generous settlement that I offered last July, I have continued to support her with a liberal personal allowance, a staff of six servants, complete maintenance of my estate at Old Westbury, Long Island, where she lives, and all expenses for my son, Searle."

"You see," Eleanor Whitney says sadly, "Sonny missed the whole point. He thought I wanted more out of him but all I wanted was him. And as far as his statement of generosity was concerned, it wasn't all glitter and gold. My original allowance was $3,500 a month. In a fit of pique he cut it to $300 a month, took half of his employees off his payroll (forcing me to pay them) and even ordered his farm workers not to supply the household with food."

The separation suit—because of legal technicalities—was a double-edged sword. Although Eleanor Whitney's intention was to maintain her marriage, separation proceedings had to include the legal attachment of her husband's New York State properties: the 1,000-acre Old Westbury estate, which included the $1.5 million mansion Sonny had built on it, a 100,000-acre preserve in the Adirondacks, a fourteen-room duplex apartment in Manhattan, as well as all other assets he owned in the area. But in addition to these monetary deterrents, the separation suit endeavored to prove that Sonny Whitney was a legal resident of New York and, if he wanted a divorce, he should seek one in his own state.

The repercussions of Eleanor Whitney's separation suit reached all the way to Las Vegas, where Whitney plunged into seclusion, but not before slashing his hitherto generous allowance.

"It was a painful dilemma for me," Eleanor Whitney remembers. "I couldn't possibly maintain a $1.5 million house— not to mention the grounds, the help, myself and my son—on $300 a month. Sonny was just being willful and nasty. My lawyers advised me to ask for temporary alimony when the separation suit reached the courts. They suggested $15,000 a week and $150,000 counsel fees." She smiles. "Even I thought that was a little outrageous but my lawyers insisted. The enormity of it, they thought, might bring Sonny to his senses. I was too numb to do anything but accept advice."

"Oh, Sonny was having his problems too. He loved this girl and he wanted to marry her and I was making it very difficult for him."

Frustrated by the legal complications, Whitney, after completing his six-week residence requirement, failed to make his expected appearance in court to ask for the divorce. Through his press agent he announced that he would not seek a divorce at present, but would attempt to reach a settlement with his wife in the hope of avoiding a court fight.

Following this retreat from the divorce courts, there was a period of supercharged waiting. Then, after a New York court order declaring Whitney a legal resident of the Empire State (a decision that would make his fourth marriage illegal), the bomb burst. Swiftly, Whitney got his divorce and immediately remarried.

To the press phalanx that descended on her Old Westbury grounds, his abandoned mate said, "He's still my husband. I have not agreed to this divorce and I am confident that our New York courts will protect my marriage and my son."

Her attorneys advised her that she could institute bigamy proceedings against her husband and stood a fair chance of having him convicted on the charge.

"It was the thing I wanted least. I didn't want to put Sonny in jail. I had no desire for revenge. I wasn't vindictive. . . . I had tried to hold him and I had failed. That was good enough for me. The statement I had made when I heard of the Nevada divorce was the spontaneous reaction of a hurt wife. But the fact that he had gone through with the divorce —despite the possible penalties—convinced me that this was what he wanted. . . . And if he wanted it so badly, he deserved to have it."

From there on in, Eleanor Whitney let her lawyers take over. The result was a $3 million settlement—second only to that made by Winthrop Rockefeller to his wife "Bobo." Two million of it went to Eleanor Whitney in outright cash. She received another $500,000 in jewels. Their thirteen-year-old son, Searle, was the beneficiary of a $205,000 trust fund. And the remaining quarter of a million dollars was to be realized in property, furniture and art objects.

"I had to make Sonny's fourth marriage kosher," she says, "so I had to sue *him* for divorce. It was a cut-and-dried formality which I went through in the state of Alabama. I can't say that I had any feelings about it. The arrangements had been made by the lawyers. All I had to do was go through the motions. . . . Oh, don't misunderstand me. It wasn't bad. Thank God, I had made peace with myself." She laughs—genuinely. "In a way, I considered myself a kind of marriage broker for Sonny's fourth plunge. I honestly hoped he would survive it. I still do. Maybe this wife has him in the right time of his life."

The nine years since then have relegated the affair to past personal history. Now she literally travels the length and breadth of the country and circles the globe to share the treasure of her faith. Her speaking engagements run into the hundreds every year and she is equally at home talking to a church group in Biloxi, Mississippi, or appearing as a speaker at the annual Presidential Prayer Breakfast in Washington, D.C. Her approach to Christianity is positive, tinged sometimes with pugnacity. She doesn't hesitate to chastise the "push-button Christians" who ring the bell for God only when they're in trouble. And she had a caustic word for those whom she calls the "Sitting Bull Christians"—the ones who sit around and shoot the bull about golf scores, fashions and what's for dinner.

"Good Lord!" she says with exasperation. "They should be talking about the good Lord . . . about His love and His place for them in eternity."

As for Eleanor Whitney, a woman not unlike millions of others who have endured heartaches, she has found her comfort in God and can't sit still for the joy and excitement of it.

JIM VAUS

Electronics and the Highest Power

THERE IS an area in New York City that is so notorious for its crime, its ghetto living conditions, its juvenile delinquency, its squalor and its hopelessness that it defies the convenience of one descriptive name. Unlike the "Village," the old "Hell's Kitchen," the "Silk Stocking District" and the "Lower East Side," which immediately evoke the character and flavor of the New York neighborhoods, this jungle of viciousness, deprivation and filth has no fewer than four aliases: "East Harlem," "Spanish Harlem," "Hell Gate Station" and the "23rd Precinct." But all four of these designations fail to describe this square mile of hell that imprisons 200,000 people and has the highest rate of crime for the smallest geographical area anywhere in this hemisphere.

Although many American cities concede responsibility for neighborhoods where it "isn't safe to walk at night," Spanish Harlem, in the early sixties, had the mournful distinction of being indifferently safe for whites—and residents too—to walk during the *day*. The area boiled with the nervous ambience of dope addiction, prostitution, burglary and juvenile warfare that raged constantly and indiscriminately among its more than forty organized gangs.

Spanish Harlem, the eastern area of this notorious ghetto, a testament to the horrors a large city can spawn, has become a ghetto within a ghetto. First came the Southern Negroes. They moved into a down-at-the-heels residential area abandoned by the whites and, subject to overcrowding, unemployment and discrimination, they watched it turn into a festering slum. The Puerto Ricans and the Cubans who followed were edged into the even less desirable areas. The gulf between the areas boils with the emotional chemicals of the slum mixture—misunderstanding, racial and language differences, and competition for jobs. Neglected equally by the white world outside, both groups take their frustrations out on each other in unresolved internecine hostility.

"It's the kind of place," a veteran social worker will explain, "where the police wait for the shooting to stop before they make the scene. If anyone else makes the scene—with or without shooting—he's either looking for trouble or he's plain out of his mind."

But James Arthur Vaus, Jr., was neither looking for trouble nor out of his mind. True, he had come a long way from the verdant countryside of Oregon, to take up life in Spanish Harlem, and, on the face of it, the social worker's assessment of such a man might seem valid. But Jim Vaus was a very special kind of man who had lived a very special kind of life and those who knew him could vouch for his sanity and his intentions.

He readily admits that the slum of Spanish Harlem at first repelled him. The people were strange to him; they were poor, many sick and untidy. The area reeked of depression and squalor. But Vaus remained because it was his Christian duty to evangelize and to try to bring to its young people a life with Christian purpose.

"At the time," he confesses, "I didn't consider Spanish Harlem my life's work. I thought the job was a challenge—the biggest one I ever tackled—but it would only be a temporary chore for me. As soon as I got my rehabilitation center started and proved it would work, I'd turn it over to others who would keep it going."

Big Jim Vaus chuckles. He pushes himself away from his desk and walks over to the window, which looks out over the

squalid back yards, the garbage cans and the populated clothes-
lines soaking up soot with sun. "I'm like 'The Man Who Came to
Dinner,' " he says.

To the residents of Spanish Harlem he must have seemed as
exotic as they seemed to him. The contrast was unavoidable—a
lumbering white giant in the land of the dark-skinned small people, Jim was over six feet tall, weighed almost 270 pounds, had
pronounced Scandinavian features, a ruddy complexion, wavy
light hair and blue eyes with a metallic glint in them.

From somewhere in the front of the "House on Second Avenue," a name that Jim Vaus had given to his rehabilitation center, came the hum of an electric motor. It was operated by one of
Spanish Harlem's "Unreachables." That's what they called the
boys who had been rejected by the city's social agencies. No one
could do anything with these problem kids. No one could even
get near them. But the "Unreachables" were what Jim Vaus
wanted. They made up the hard core of the gang fighters, the
street killers, the muggers. If the ever-spiraling crime rate in
Spanish Harlem was to be checked, the "Unreachables" had to be
reached.

"Frankly, we didn't think he had a ghost of a chance." These
words summed up the reaction of the social workers and the police officials of the 23rd Precinct. "After all, what did he have
going for him? He wasn't a social worker. He had no experience
with the hardened juvenile delinquent. And, besides, he was more
than an outsider as far as Spanish Harlem was concerned. He
wasn't even a New Yorker."

Vaus's credentials, as far as they could see, were his convictions, his belief in the redeeming power of Jesus Christ, his gifts
as an electronics engineer and his criminal prison record. The last
was paradoxically a strong asset, because a known convicted criminal, a close associate of the notorious gambler Mickey Cohen, a
former member of a crime syndicate, possessed undeniable social
status among young hoods. Jim Vaus had been all of these and
more.

"More is right. Much more," Jim Vaus volunteers. "No use forgetting the stretch I did at the McNeil Island Federal Penitentiary. That was for misusing government priorities and misappropriating government property. I was in the Army then and a captain to boot. And just to complete the record, there were a couple of jobs I pulled in my youth too."

Jim Vaus was going back a number of years; to his school days and a little beyond. The school was the Bible Institute in Los Angeles. It was his father's choice rather than his own. But Jim's father was a preacher and his fondest hope was to have his son follow in his footsteps. At the Institute, Jim studied Hebrew, Greek, church history and all the related subjects that were designed to prepare a young man for the ministry. Young Vaus would have preferred science and especially electronics. But he did well enough at the Institute to earn a scholarship to Wheaton, a Christian college in Illinois.

The prospect of being away from home and seeing some of the world was irresistible, and inspired his transfer from the Bible Institute. His stay at Wheaton was undistinguished by any pursuit of higher learning. His major was fun and games. His only "accomplishment" was a wire-tapping job, executed in the girls' dormitory. The record playback was a campus howl. Since wiretapping was not an accredited course at Wheaton, and his academic record was listless, he was asked to leave.

So it was back to the Bible Institute in Los Angeles. The charming and clever prodigal found swift welcome. His classmates elected him treasurer of the Bible Institute's *Annual*. The money that came in from advertising and book sales went into a bank account under his name. But more than that, Jim handled the funds for the hundred-voice chorus, which made weekly radio appearances. Sometimes the chorus expenses would be late coming through. Then Jim would borrow the money from the *Annual*'s bank account. It was the beginning of a fund-juggling career at the Institute.

This was the time of the Great Depression and money for

the annual publication was scarce. Advertising and book orders weren't materializing. To fill the monetary void, the Institute held a fund-raising rally. It was a dismal failure.

"By then," Jim Vaus confesses, "I was so far behind in my accounts that in one wild, illogical moment I withdrew the Institute money from the bank and took a plane to Florida."

It was an act of panic by the young man. Fortunately, it passed quickly and before long Jim was back in Los Angeles, confessing his guilt and promising full restitution. In order to accomplish the latter, he had to borrow the money, signing a note for his debt. The Institute didn't press charges. With the return of the money, it was content to drop the matter. But it also dropped Jim Vaus. He was expelled with a warning from the dean to stay away not only from the Institute but from the students as well.

With this black mark on his record, Jim Vaus had no choice but to forget about school and try his luck in the business world. He took a job as a wrapper in a large Los Angeles department store. The pay was inadequate. He couldn't afford the pleasures he enjoyed or the people he would like to call his friends. Even his hobbies were on the extravagant side. He puts it this way: "As far back as grammar-school days I was interested in radio. During my high-school period, I studied everything that would help me master the subject. I built a ham radio station in the second story of our garage. It was super fun but, of course, it was an expensive hobby. That's the kind I always had."

In a vaguely rationalistic manner he reasoned that his urge for money originated with the fact that he came from a poor family. In fair truth, his family was not poor but average middle class. Although money had not been one of his preacher father's foremost pursuits, his family lived in modest security. But their mode of living was hardly sumptuous and anything less than sumptuous seemed grinding for young Jim. He blamed his "poverty" on the fact that his father was a Christian preacher and it became convenient to make Christianity synonymous with drabness.

It was this nagging rationalization of deprivation that

helped drive him to his second act of crime. Borrowing both his father's "ancient" car and his old, rusty .32-caliber revolver, he committed an armed robbery. The stickup wasn't very lucrative. It netted him a measly fourteen dollars and a four-year jail sentence. Thanks to the intervention of family and friends, the prison term was reduced to one year in jail and three years' probation.

That one prison year was a paradox for Vaus. For someone who so loved the gay, free life, incarceration would have to press down hard. Yet the prison farm with its healthy outdoor details seemed associated with safety and the obviation of trouble. He endured the sentence with dislike, not horror, and not without some periods of inner reflection. However, the day of release was a blissful nirvana.

"There is no feeling in all the world like that tremendous moment of release," he recalls. "The world seems to stop spinning and you step onto the sidewalk—a free man! I've lived many a top moment, but release is the moment of all moments."

He didn't even mind, a month after his freedom from prison, being drafted into the Army of World War II. In the fervid post-Pearl Harbor days, khaki was the proudest color in the world. Because of a probation technicality, in his armed-robbery escapade he had been officially declared "Not Guilty." He was eligible for induction and his superior intelligence made him automatic officer-candidate material.

As a lieutenant, Vaus was assigned to an antiaircraft battalion in Los Angeles. Vaus's naturally inherited gifts for electronics brought him into the challenge of how the newly discovered radar system could refine antiaircraft effectiveness. To correctly aim and fire one antiaircraft gun—even with radar—required the services of three men. Vaus became convinced that this situation could be improved. He spent his off-duty hours tinkering with the radar equipment; testing it, refining it until he came up with a mechanism that would both calculate and aim the gun. All that was needed was one man to fire it. The results so impressed the commanding general of the 37th Brigade that Lieutenant Vaus was elevated to the rank of captain and given the "go-ahead."

Aside from the personal pleasure he derived from his "good job, well done" and his promotion, Jim Vaus was pleased for his family's sake. This would prove to them that he had indeed undergone reformation and was making good. Unlike the miser who hugs material success to himself as he withdraws from the world, Jim Vaus's personality expanded. He literally exuded generosity. Let any fellow officer find himself in need of a priority for photographic equipment, and Jim Vaus was always ready and willing to oblige. It might not have been SOP (Standard Operating Procedure) but it was downright human procedure. In Jim's book, it hurt no one and it made nice guys more comfortable.

But even the best-intentioned ointments are not devoid of flies and in this case the "fly" turned out to be an officer who was jealous of Jim's accomplishments and his rapid rise in rank. The man reported Jim's priority gifts to the commanding officer, and an investigation followed. It was during this investigation that the Board of Inquiry turned up an unauthorized Army projector in Jim's possession. He was using the projector for experimental rather than private purposes but this fact was not considered a mitigating condition. Captain Jim Vaus was court-martialed. The verdict was "Guilty" and he was sentenced to a term of ten years in a federal penitentiary. Even Vaus's fellow officers agreed that the sentence was out of proportion to the crime. There followed a period of waiting while the Vaus case was being reviewed. But the verdict of the review board didn't measure up to Jim's hope. His sentence was cut in half—five years instead of ten—and he was shipped off to the McNeil Island Federal Penitentiary to serve it out.

In those early days of his second imprisonment, Jim wondered about the vagaries of justice. Granted, he was a criminal in the eyes of the Army, but weren't those officers who had asked for and received the G.I. gifts just as guilty as he? It was a futile question, the kind a convicted bookmaker might ask about his former patrons.

The five-year sentence was terminated in five months. Japan

had surrendered and World War II was over. Then the President of the United States, Harry S. Truman, reviewed his case. This time the verdict was a complete pardon and Vaus was shipped out to Fort Leavenworth for a rehabilitation period. He was free and, officially, no longer a criminal. Because of his wide knowledge of radar and his experience, he was assigned to the Air Force and toured the country with a group of officers to speak at colleges and universities, explaining the mysteries of this new miraculous detecting device.

His tour of duty ended in a year. He was given an honorable discharge and walked out of the Army firmly convinced that he was about to start a new and different life; no more checkered careers, no more ups and downs in rank and especially no more ins and outs of jail.

Vaus smiles wryly when he thinks back to that time. "Little did I know what lay ahead of me. All I planned to do was go into business for myself, open my 'Electronics Engineering Consultants' firm and put out the best damn custom-built radio in the world."

The ostensibly finished business of trouble and the preparation for a new life involved a lady friend who had serious intentions of marrying the young engineer. The shame of Vaus's escapades proved to be too much for them both; the romance withered and died. After a short period of remorse, Vaus met a tall, willowy brunette with the freshly scrubbed ingenuous features of a college cheerleader, and this romance took. After an eighteen-month courtship, Alice became Mrs. Vaus.

The future looked bright for the young couple. The free-wheeling giant with the quick intelligence, the charm of a born salesman and the phenomenal talent was a shoo-in for big-money success in the posh environs of the Los Angeles community. Everybody was happy: the elder Vauses in their parsonage, because their son seemed to have straightened out with the community; the new Mrs. Vaus in their charming new house with the shiny new car and with the prospect of a child to occupy the nursery.

His electronics-engineering business had made an auspicious start. For the most part he was designing and installing elaborate electronic equipment for the wealthier members of the Los Angeles community. In one house alone he had installed a custom-built radio with outlets in twenty rooms, a complete intercom system along with electrically wired gates and garage doors, and a ring of trespass-control lights around its thirteen-acre estate. In addition to his private contracts, he was doing work for the aircraft industry, developing electronic-component systems. He made a lot of money swiftly, spent it on good living and worried little that the ascent would falter.

To help out an invalid friend who owned an apartment house, Jim took over the temporary management of the property. It was one of the better apartment houses in Hollywood—quiet, well kept and, for the most part, occupied by respectable, prosperous tenants. The one exception was a suspected prostitute who was operating on the premises. It didn't concern Vaus as long as she didn't upset the tenants. But as her clientele increased, the tenants complained. Some of them threatened to move. Vaus called the police.

The three vice-squad detectives who appeared explained that they needed evidence to make an arrest.

"I'm afraid we're stymied, Mr. Vaus," they said. "We know there are men going in and out of her apartment but we can't see or hear what's going on. We can't do a thing unless we have something substantial to go on."

Vaus was amazed that the police were not equipped to gather evidence except by breaking-down-the-door raids. Such an obvious lack in the police department of a major city challenged the professional electronics engineer. The morals involved concerned him little. This was purely an exercise in ingenuity. He worked on the problem most of the night and when the detectives returned the next day, he was ready for them. He had concealed a microphone in the girl's apartment, connected with a wire that ran to a recording machine in his own room, and that was that.

The vice-squad detectives had their evidence that led to a conviction, and the apartment house was rid of its nuisance.

As far as Vaus was concerned it was a minor experience with no implications for the future. But in a week the vice-squad men were back, this time with a proposition. Would he work with the police on a consultant basis, using his electronics knowhow to help the department break its really tough cases involving gamblers as well as prostitutes?

The idea fascinated him; especially when the detectives explained what they were after. "Let's put it this way, Mr. Vaus," they explained. "Let's say John Doe walks into a drugstore and uses a particular booth to dial a number and place a bet on a horse in the fifth race at Santa Anita. Could you set up a device, or a system, so that the officer working on the case could not only listen in on the conversation but determine the telephone number of the bookie who was being called? If you can do it, we can break the bookmaking racket in this town."

Jim Vaus thought it could be done. Again, it was a professional challenge. He had nothing against bookmakers or, for that matter, the bookmakers' clientele. Breaking the bookmakers might have been a police ambition, but his ambition was to make an electronics breakthrough and a fee. He went to work on the problem and came up with a device that is known as the "impulse indicator." Along with the impulse indicator—which is now a standard piece of detection equipment widely used by police, sheriffs' offices and federal agencies across the country—he designed equipment that made it possible for an officer to listen in on a telephone conversation without any physical contact with the line. All the man needed to know was the originating telephone number of the call. And once contact was made, the receiver's telephone number could easily be determined.

The Los Angeles police department was jubilant. As a result of the Vaus wizardry, a big damper frustrated the bookies. They were fearful of using the telephone to transact the bulk of their business. They were reduced to personal contacts, with deleterious effects on their income. Vaus's impulse indicator, along with accompanying equipment, also helped smash the call-girl empire of Brenda Allen, the notorious Hollywood madam-procurer.

The Brenda Allen case made headlines all over the country, reaching as high as the U.S. Senate and the Kefauver Investigating Committee in its probe of vice and corruption throughout the country. Jim Vaus's role in this turmoil was, of necessity, brought to light. It was nothing to be ashamed of (after all, he was working on the side of the law) but he emerged from all the notoriety as the nation's ace wire-tapper. Soon after the Brenda Allen case, he was approached by movie star Mickey Rooney and his manager.

"We understand, Mr. Vaus, that it's possible for you to listen in on a telephone conversation without making a connection with the telephone line and without going anywhere near the residence. Is that true?"

Jim Vaus was wary. He didn't know what the actor and his manager were driving at. "Yes, that's true. I can do it. What do you have in mind?"

The manager pulled out a five-hundred-dollar bill from his wallet. "Mr. Vaus, if you tap the telephone line of Crestwood 6-9451 in the next five minutes and make a recording of the conversation, this five-hundred-dollar bill is yours."

For a big man, Jim Vaus could move quickly when the stakes were high. He set up his equipment and, using the same technique he had employed for the Los Angeles Police Department, he had a tap on the Rooney telephone line in less than five minutes. He let Rooney and his manager listen in on a telephone conversation between the actor's Philippine houseboy and his bookie. It was an amusing curtain raiser. The main performance was not far behind. In a few minutes Rooney's wife was on the phone in an amorous conversation with a strange man.

This was the evidence the actor wanted. He had had his suspicions and was thinking about a divorce but he wasn't sure—not until then. Now he had the evidence, all wrapped up in an incriminating recorded telephone conversation. Mickey Rooney paid Jim off handsomely. But it was a bargain for the actor because Jim Vaus's little job made it possible for Rooney to obtain a divorce without adhering to the equal-division-of-property clause in the California divorce law. This could be waived only when the circumstances were unusual; in other words, when incriminating evidence could be produced which would brand a mate unfaithful.

In a town like Hollywood, word of such talent travels fast. It wasn't long before Vaus was making thousands of dollars wiretapping and recording extracurricular love conversations for a host of movie stars, among them Errol Flynn, Dick Haymes and Xavier Cugat. The element Jim liked most about his new-found career was that it was foolproof as far as collections were concerned. He often thought about it—even at church services, which he still attended regularly. Often he would sit in his pew, as the minister droned on, and relish his enviable position. The commodity he sold—the recorded wire taps—was in great demand and if the party of the first part complained about the fee, he could always sell it for more to the party of the second part.

As time wore on, Jim Vaus's wire-tapping business expanded with his reputation. He no longer devoted himself exclusively to police and divorce work. Big business and political organizations solicited his services. He wire-tapped and recorded for all of them, stealing secrets and secret plans from competitors and opponents. . . . And then, when he thought he had touched all bases, he got the surprise of his life—a call from the notorious gambler Mickey Cohen.

The Mickey Cohen of those days was a far cry from the crippled prison inmate of today. (Cohen is presently serving out an income-tax-evasion conviction. He is a chronic invalid, the result of a vicious beating he received at the hands of a fellow convict who had gone berserk.) The old Mickey Cohen of the early postwar days was a flashy figure. Jim Vaus describes him this way: "Seated behind a large circular desk in his walnut-paneled office in the rear of his plush haberdashery shop, he made quite an impression. He was short, stocky, solidly built. His tailoring was exquisite, his grooming impeccable. Not a hair was out of place. His round face was serious—even a little sad. But most outstanding were his eyes. These were like two miniature cameras —focusing, flashing, snapping sharp, indelible pictures for his personal album."

The gambler was quick to put his cards on the table. He told Jim Vaus that he was certain the police had planted a microphone in his house. He wanted it found and destroyed. He thought Jim was the only man for the job.

"Mr. Cohen, you've got me all wrong." At that moment Jim had no intention of working for Hollywood's gambling czar. "My business is installing microphones, not taking them out."

Mickey Cohen smiled mirthlessly. He reached into his pocket and pulled out a roll of hundred-dollar bills. The dimensions of this wad were calculated to dampen even the most stubborn resistance. With deliberate significance, he peeled off three bills and placed them on the desk.

That kind of money broke Vaus's resistance fast. He took on the job. It was more complex than Cohen had envisioned. The police microphone had been cleverly hidden. But with the use of a high-gain amplifier and an ultrasensitive pickup, Vaus was able to track it down, buried under an inch and a half of subflooring. He extracted the microphone, an amplifier and yards of wiring that linked Cohen's house to an outside line and a receiver in downtown police headquarters.

Mickey was impressed. He looked at the array of gadgetry spread out before him and gave Jim his hand; cupped within it was a bonus of three one-hundred-dollar bills.

"Vaus, how would you like to have a permanent job with me?"

Jim hesitated. He wasn't poverty stricken. He had his electronics business, his work for the police department and his wiretapping jobs for the movie colony. Yet he knew that all three of these activities paid off in peanuts compared to what the steady payoff of one solid connection with Mickey Cohen might be. But there was the deterrent of being "outside the law," and for a man with Jim Vaus's background this was a psychological factor hard to sublimate.

The wad in his pocket radiated a promise of more creature comforts: a fine house, more luxuries, travel first class, free-and-easy living all around.

"What did you have in mind, Mr. Cohen?"

Cohen's interests were not confined to horse racing and other sporting events. Mickey was diversifying his activities. He wanted an inside ear on politics, official business and even certain commercial enterprises. Vaus was interested—provided he could keep on with his wire-tapping for the police. Cohen had no objections. If he thought it was a peculiar condition of employment, he didn't say so.

"My work with Mickey Cohen," Jim Vaus explains, "was no more sinister than it was for the police department. It was just as illegal for me to tap wires for a law-enforcement agency as it was for a gambling czar. Anyhow, the work was more important to me than the job. I was fascinated by electronics and the tricks I could do with them. I could make them defy all known physical laws and successfully hear the seemingly unhearable."

As far as his professional association with a known gambler was concerned, Jim worked with him long enough to form his own conception of the man. After a while, he realized there were two Mickey Cohens. One was caricatured by the newspapers as the "Czar of Hollywood's Gangland": a swaggering parasite who coordinated vice and corruption, a villain whose name in the headlines sold newspapers. The other Mickey Cohen was the human being he learned to know: a shrewd man but generous to a fault, who didn't smoke, drink or tell a lie; a devoted husband, a man who hungered for understanding and friendship.

For eight months Jim Vaus led a double professional life. One day he labored for the police, and the next for Mickey Cohen. Many times his anomalous position led him into touch-and-go situations which imperiled both his jobs. The fees the police paid him were trifles compared to the retainer he received from Cohen. After a while it became obvious that this job juggling couldn't go on. He would have to make a choice, and the choice wasn't too difficult. Gradually, he eased himself out of his police work. Whenever the law called for his services, he became "too busy." Eventually the break with the police was clean and Vaus moved his offices into the building that housed Mickey Cohen's haberdashery shop.

It was here, and through Mickey Cohen, that he met a big-time gambler who was everything Mickey was touted to be but wasn't. Andy was a stereotype of the underworld: short, shifty, swarthy. He reminded Jim of a thin stick of dynamite awaiting a fuse.

"Heard a lot about you, Vaus," he told Jim at their first meeting. "Mickey tells me you make a lot of swell listening gadgets for him. How about doing something for me?"

"Like what?" Jim wanted to know.

"Like beating the Continental Wire Service by a minute and a half."

Jim had heard about the Continental Wire Service. It transmitted racing results to major cities from tracks all over the country. Bookmakers headed its list of subscribers. If Jim could devise a method that would delay the results from reaching the bookies' teletypewriters by a minute and a half, Andy's boys—stationed in the bookmaking parlors—would receive a call telling them when a long shot came in. In that minute-and-a-half lag, the boys could place their whopping big bets and just wait around to collect their money. It was a foolproof system, especially if you concentrated on horses that paid twenty to one or over.

It took Jim Vaus four months to solve the problem of the minute-and-a-half lag. He did it with a combination of teletypewriter equipment and electronic components. They tried it in Nevada first. Jim located the Continental Wire line and plugged in on it. Then he inserted a ninety-second delay when the results started coming through. If a long shot registered, Andy called a confederate who was waiting at a local bookie parlor. He told him which horse had won and how much to play on it. It was less trouble than going to the bank. In that first trial run they almost put one Nevada bookie out of business.

"Vaus, you're a genius!" Andy said, and they went on to give the Jim Vaus delay system another trial; this time in Arizona. Here the results were even more impressive. Jim and Andy were able to cut down the transaction time—from the inserted delay to the placing of the bet—by ten seconds.

Andy was jubilant. "That does it, Vaus. We're ready to go big time now."

By "big time" Andy meant they could blanket a section of the country instead of an isolated city or state. They could set up headquarters in Saint Louis and control every race west of the Mississippi.

"You know what your cut is, Vaus. You'll be a millionaire in six months."

"OK, it's a deal."

"Great! Meet me next week and we'll settle the details. Then off we go to the gold mines of Saint Louis."

In the seven days that followed, Vaus suffered the dilemmas of a man torn. Half the time he exulted, visualizing the riches that lay ahead of him: a millionaire in six months, a *pâté de foie gras* life, with security and a termination to his lifelong obsessive complex of living on the fringes of poverty. His other half juggled doubts and fears. What if they were caught? It would mean jail again.

Such conflicts he never shared with Alice. Although she worried about his odd hours, his free-and-easy ways and his occasional contacts with unorthodox cronies, he was never really in trouble. He provided well, loved his growing family and never denied his wife the fruits of his earnings. Besides, it was easy for any husband to shoo away a wife's doubts when his work activities involved such complexities as electronics. He did that job fairly well, but not well enough to erase completely the apprehensive instinct of his sensitive mate. Vaus was then, as he is now, possessed of a powerful and persuasive intellect. If doubt assails his conscience, he seldom demonstrates it openly. He conducts his approaches to human conduct with the empirical certitude of his concentration and knowledge of scientific fact. He is not easily swung over, moved about or reconvinced. In total impact he projects the image of the cerebral man whose mind is accustomed to mastery over his emotions.

At the end of his private dialogue, he told himself that it was silly to worry, to borrow trouble when you had this big a proposition going for you. Besides, at that particular time, there seemed to be a de-emphasis on crime and vice in the press; not only in Los Angeles but throughout the country. Fickle journalism was turning from sin to salvation, and Billy Graham was becoming the hit parade of the fourth estate. This "Billy Sunday" of Jim Vaus's generation was standing them in the aisles. His Canvas Cathedral on the outskirts of Los Angeles was packing them in every night; ten thousand came, stood in the aisles, spilled out into the night just to listen to this colorful preacher. Even *Life, Look,* and *Time* were giving generous space to this unprecedented religious revival.

Jim Vaus read all the accounts of the Billy Graham meetings with wry amusement. He noted that more than five thousand people had "made their decision for Christ" at Billy Graham's Canvas Cathedral. Some of them were celebrities: Louis Zamperini, the former Olympic track star, Harvey Fitts, who was TV's "Colonel Zack" . . . and Stuart Hamblen. When Jim saw Hamblen's name and the headline "SINGER STUART HAMBLEN HITS SAWDUST TRAIL AT REVIVAL," he said to himself, "Oh, no! What that guy won't do for publicity!"

He knew all about Hamblen—his cowboy singing, his drinking bouts, his carousing and his string of race horses. The last time he had read about Hamblen, the man was picked up drunk and disorderly. Now there was this business about conversion. It was more than Vaus could accept. Certainly he felt no impulse to emulate Hamblen. His own religious traditions had been delivered to him sans complications. From the pietistic atmosphere of the parsonage home through two religious colleges,

Vaus had heard the Word hammered at him. As a bright, inquiring young intellectual, he had constructed all the arguments against religion and had engaged in exercises of logic with parents and teachers to demolish their beliefs. But after maturity the compulsion to disbelieve faded; his spiritual personality remained in suspension. If his current life played a discordant strain to the hymn of faith, then he would much prefer it to what seemed like the drab, antiscientific, joyless life within the church. So he remained outside of it, in control of his mind, holding at bay whatever urgings from the heart might bring him closer to the faith of his origins.

These concerns melted when he met again with Andy.

"I'm all set, Vaus. I got my boys alerted. I got the bookie joints marked for the kill. How are you fixed? Ready to go?"

"I'm ready, Andy. All I have to do is ship my equipment and take off."

"Fine. Ship it air freight. I'm in a hurry. Here. . . ." Andy's hand went to his pocket and came out with a roll of bills. "Expense money, Jim. Live it up. You may as well get used to the good things in life. They could be with you for a long time." Then he laughed and monotoned the words of an old song: "See you in Saint Louis, Louis."

When Jim Vaus started for home that night, he switched on his car radio. Stuart Hamblen and his Lucky Starrs were coming in strong. . . . But even Jim Vaus could tell that this was a different Stuart Hamblen. He was singing hymns instead of hillbilly songs. But more important, he was knocking his sponsors instead of praising them. Cigarette smoking was dangerous, he told his listeners. Beer drinking was the insidious road to alcoholism, he said.

"I'll be damned!" Jim Vaus said to himself. "If he keeps this up, he won't have a nickel to his name."

And then there came the clincher. Jim Vaus could hardly believe his ears.

"A few nights ago," Stuart Hamblen was saying, "I heard Billy Graham preach, and I accepted Christ as my personal Savior. Since then my life has been changed completely. I am selling my stable of seven race horses. I am keeping El Lobo [his big $50,000 stakes winner] but only for sentimental reasons. I will never race him again."

Jim Vaus flipped off the radio. . . . "Well," he said to himself, "this guy isn't kidding. If Stuart Hamblen is selling his race horses, he's for real. . . . There couldn't be anything behind it. This couldn't be a publicity stunt."

It was a disturbing admission for Jim Vaus to make. As a matter of fact, he began to realize that this whole Billy Graham Los Angeles revival was disturbing him. He was experiencing vague stirrings: memories of his Christian childhood, echoes of his father's words and his father's teachings. He shrugged them off but not without effort. He busied himself putting his equipment in shape and shipping it off to Saint Louis. There were a couple of days to wait before he himself would board a plane to meet Andy and get to work. But one of those days was a Sunday, and an idle Sunday, in Jim's state of mind, was a difficult one to get through. He thought he might make it pass quickly if he spent some time with his friends. He tried one bar after the other. No one was around. Some were in the country, others on fishing trips, golf dates. Even Mickey Cohen was off somewhere on a "business trip."

With nothing else to do, Jim decided to take a drive. He didn't know where or what for. He just got into his car and took off. He was driving along Los Angeles' Washington Boulevard when he suddenly realized he was heading straight for Billy Graham's Canvas Cathedral. He was about to turn off when he said to himself, "Why not? Let's see what all this hullabaloo is all about."

The hullabaloo involved 10,000 people trying to crowd into a tent that was capable of seating no more than about 6,200. The best Jim was able to do was an aisle seat on a bench at the back of the tent. It was good enough for him. He was here solely as an observer—not as a participant. The surroundings impressed him little. Neither the hymns, the sawdust floor, nor the inelegantly dressed crowd moved him to anything but memory that Christians, especially the full gospel types, always looked so drably turned out.

Then Billy Graham appeared. He stepped to the center of the platform. Although Vaus's reaction was not negative, it was also hardly positive. The best he could muster was, "I couldn't find anything wrong with him." Yet he couldn't ignore the sincere conviction of this preacher: his movements, his voice, his ease that was born of assurance.

Graham's words weren't new to Jim Vaus. They were the same words his father had used, the same words hundreds of preachers had used hundreds of yesterdays. But there was a difference. The sincerity of this preacher was coming through. No jokes, no gimmicks. This was all Christ, all Christian. It was the core, the essence, the truth of Christianity, the literal Holy Bible.

"Somewhere in this great audience tonight," Billy Graham was saying, "there is a man who has heard this story many times before. This man knows that now is the time for him to make his decision for Christ. But, as he has done so often in the past, he is saying 'no' to God. He is hardening his heart, stiffening his neck and planning to leave this place without Christ. . . ."

It was as though Billy Graham were talking not to the thousands around him but to Jim Vaus himself. And Jim Vaus was indeed hardening his heart against Christ. He was telling himself that to accept Christ now was a luxury he couldn't afford. It would cost him a small fortune if he backed out of the gambling syndicate. He certainly couldn't work for Christ and Andy. Then there was the real threat of personal violence if he did back out. Andy and his boys wouldn't take kindly to a welsher; especially if the welsher was Jim Vaus, who—along with his mystical electronic equipment—was the very heart of the bookie-beating scheme. They'd just as soon kill him as look at him.

The words of a hymn the crowd had sung passed through his mind: "Almost persuaded not to believe, almost persuaded Christ to receive."

Billy Graham's counselors were moving up and down the

aisles, scanning the faces of the crowd; touching a shoulder, reaching out for a hand, inviting a vacillating member to go forward and declare himself for Christ. For some reason the counselors aggravated Jim Vaus. He guessed it was because he didn't like anyone butting in on someone's private religious business. He swore that if any one of those nosy-bodies touched him, he'd let him have it. A wizened little man approached and took Jim's hand. It was "Uncle" Billy Scholfield, one of Graham's most enthusiastic counselors. Uncle Billy was about to invite Vaus to go forward when he saw the look on the man's face. He said nothing; just held fast to Jim's hand, bowed his head and began to pray.

Jim Vaus vividly recalls those moments in the Canvas Cathedral with Uncle Billy praying over him. "I felt like hitting the old guy. But you can't hit a man when he's praying. So I bit my lip and waited. . . . And as I waited and listened to him pray, something strange began to happen to me. For one thing, I stopped wanting to hit the old man. For another, I began to feel a kind of softness enveloping me. It was as though my belligerence and my resistance to Christ were being dissolved by some mysterious chemical agent. . . . No, I wasn't breaking down and giving in. I was a young man. I had plenty of time to make my decision for Christ. When I got older and had my pile stashed away, I'd straighten out my life. . . . Plenty of time and plenty of chances. . . ."

Then Billy Graham was speaking again. He was standing on the platform hundreds of feet away, but his words were answering Jim Vaus's thoughts.

"You know, friends," Graham was saying, "you just can't decide for Christ whenever you want to. The only time a man can decide for Christ is when the Holy Spirit of God has brought conviction to his heart. Friends, if God is bringing conviction to your heart tonight, you dare not say 'no.' He may never again give you this opportunity. . . . *This is your moment of decision."*

Those were the very words that brought conversion to Jim

Vaus. "Something within me broke," he says. "I turned to Uncle Billy Scholfield and said, 'OK. I'll go.' "

He went down the aisle and knelt in the sawdust. All around him were earnest Christians talking and praying with those who had come forward.

"Lord," he said, "I believe this time from the bottom of my heart. . . . The road ahead for me is a rough one. It's going to be almost impossible to straighten out this bewildered, tangled life of mine. But if You'll straighten it out, I'll turn it over to You—all of it."

The next morning the Los Angeles papers headlined Jim's conversion: "WIRE-TAPPER VAUS HITS SAWDUST TRAIL." He was in the same class with Stuart Hamblen, Louis Zamperini and Colonel Zack—the celebrities whom everyone doubted. But that wasn't Jim's concern. He didn't care if everyone in the world doubted him. For the first time in his life he no longer doubted himself. Now what he doubted was his ability to stay alive, once he told Andy that the Saint Louis deal was off. But he couldn't flinch from this ordeal—no matter what the cost.

The call that Jim made to Andy in Saint Louis went according to his expectations. Andy's first reaction was disbelief. Then he thought Jim was either drunk, trying to be funny or just plain crazy. When the message finally got through to him, Andy reacted in typical gangland fashion.

"I don't like this one bit, Vaus. I got men planted all over the place. It's costing me plenty of dough. All output and no intake until we get going on this job. So you better get wise to yourself and come on out here."

Jim reiterated his stand. He was through. He was quitting. He was not going to Saint Louis.

"OK. But just remember this, Vaus. No one quits on Andy. See? If you're not coming out to Saint Louis, me and my boys will be around to see you. Understand, Vaus?"

Jim put down the phone with a sick feeling. He understood what Andy meant. No one had to spell it out for him. It would be curtains for him or, at best, they'd cripple him for life. He prayed a nervous, jerky prayer for help.

The days that followed were busy and difficult. The only thing that sustained him was his reborn belief, the Holy Bible and his attendance at Billy Graham's Canvas Cathedral. Out of all this activity one core of solid truth emerged: He had hungered for silver and searched for all the hidden treasures of electronics. Now he must seek the knowledge of God with equal zeal and dedication. . . . Restitution was a partial answer. In his devious preconversion period Jim Vaus had misappropriated and stolen $15,000 worth of electronic equipment from the local telephone company and a radio station. He sold his house and his automobile to make restitution. In an almost forgotten criminal case—in which he had offered perjured testimony which had convicted a Los Angeles police official—he petitioned the court to reopen the case for his true testimony. At the risk of a jail sentence for incriminating himself, he changed his testimony. As a result, the police official was freed. The possible perjury indictment against Vaus never materialized because his public conversion had so impressed the court that it was convinced of Jim Vaus's reformation.

Now there were only Andy and his hoods to face, and Jim Vaus waited. . . . They came in the late afternoon—a big black sedan turning into the driveway—and Andy and three of his hoods walked up to the front door, where Jim Vaus was waiting for them.

"Like I said, Vaus, we came around to see you."

"Andy, did you read about the change in my life in the newspapers?"

"Sure, sure, Vaus. I read it."

"What do you think about it, Andy?"

"I think this guy Graham must have given you a couple of grand to stand up and say you got religion. Now you got your dough, let's get going."

For forty-five minutes Jim Vaus talked to Andy and his boys. He told them about his conversion, about his new relationship with God, about his acceptance of Christ as his Savior. When he stopped speaking, Andy turned and walked back to his car. The boys followed him. Jim watched the car as it sped away. He stood for a moment, overwhelmed by the miracle of his escape.

On subsequent occasions before the public, in front of investigation commissions and on the church platform, Vaus ventilated the entire story of his career; in some cases, perforce, branding his former colleagues. And with impunity. One of them, Mickey Cohen, surprisingly congratulated him, wished him well, and even indicated his fleeting envy of Vaus's new life. Alice Vaus, faced with the loss of the house and assorted material possessions, was nothing less than relieved and delighted.

For the better part of five years Vaus worked to pay back old debts against persons and to a human society he had violated. He and his wife had decided to leave the Los Angeles area and with their three children rebuild themselves in a bucolic area of Oregon surrounded by green fields and black Angus cattle. Vaus had been making his living doing inventive electronic work and had decided to supplement their income by raising livestock so that he would have all the time he desired to travel with his electronic equipment, giving religious talks to church groups and young people and in the schools. He would cram his station wagon to the roof with the electronic gear, then set it up in an auditorium, demonstrating the mystery of man-made lightning, dizzying jumps of electricity from table to hair to fingertips. Then, having dazzled his audience, he would explain the mystic force of the universe—stemming from God, existing in complete reality although not seen unless contacted—much like the awareness in a man's heart.

On one of his tours in 1959, someone in Philadelphia urged him to visit the tragic center of Spanish Harlem in New York. He was shocked by what he saw and immediately felt an injunction to bring the message of Christ's love there. His feelings about social work without God is that it is content without form. The inspiration must come not from man to man but from God through man. A redeemed individual must do good. A do-gooder without God offers a palliative to the pain. God offers the font of endless depth.

Almost impulsively Vaus discussed the problem with the police, the discipline deans of the local schools and other interested officials. He rented a ramshackle store on 101st Street with his own money, built counters for his electronic gear, set up a cot in the rear of the rat-infested premises, where he lived alone. He rigged up a two-way TV setup so he could see the outside from within as a protective device. He wanted all the kids to come in and learn about electronics and perhaps talk about Jesus Christ. He sought out the toughest gang leaders; they got to know and trust him.

The kids of Spanish Harlem knew all about the "do-gooders." They had heard about phonies. They may not have heard about Missouri but for all intents and purposes they were natives of the "show-me" state. And Jim Vaus had to show them in order to win them. He went to bat for them by honoring their confidences. He went to bat for them by appearing in court and pleading with a judge for understanding in a car-theft case or a seemingly senseless gangland killing. In the latter case, Jim Vaus succeeded in raising $6,000 for legal fees to defend the four boys charged with murder. Although he was convinced of their guilt, he was also convinced that the second-degree murder charge against them was too severe. His lawyers were successful in having the charge reduced. So the resultant sentence was also reduced and the boys stood a chance of coming out of jail with enough of their lives to do something with.

As the months passed, it became apparent to Vaus that his temporary tenure in Spanish Harlem was to become the life's work he had been searching for. He sold his lovely home in Oregon, moved Alice and the children (there are now four) and set up permanent quarters in the East.

It is seven years since Big Jim Vaus set up shop in Spanish Harlem. In those seven years, his Youth Development Corporation has branched out. He now has three rehabilitation centers with a permanent staff of seventeen professional counselors, remedial-reading experts and a group of twenty to forty volunteer workers. The volunteers are an important factor in Big Jim's program. Their visits to the kids confined in hospital wards or prison cells maintain a human chain of reality for these disadvantaged youths who have lost contact with the outside world. The volunteers write letters for them, run errands and, most of all, remind them that someone cares enough to worry about them and their future. Never neglected is the spiritual message of Christ's redeeming power.

Five years ago Jim Vaus took a giant step in his work to make the juvenile delinquents of Spanish Harlem break out of the desperate straitjackets that doomed them to a purgatory of crime and punishment. His logic was simple. Their environment was as much to blame as their frantic instincts, he thought. It might be that their environment even gave birth to their frantic instincts. . . . If he could take them out of this ghetto of dirt and squalor, give them a taste of God's trees and grass instead of a slum lord's neglect—broken windows, backed-up toilets, garbage-strewn halls—these children might be helped to emerge as decent human beings. He thought it was worth a try.

Enlisting the moral and financial support of such people as General Dwight D. Eisenhower, President Herbert Hoover, Governor Thomas E. Dewey and George Champion of The Chase Manhattan Bank, as well as many other prominent citizens, he established his Youth Development Camp near Port Jervis, New York. The total cost was $750,000. It paid for 350 rolling green acres, a group of superbly constructed camp buildings and a staff of counselors whose job was to discover the latent talents of these children, encourage these talents and give them a sense of responsibility to the work they were best fitted for. A two-week vacation is free for everyone.

The Youth Development project has been a tremendous success; not because all the displaced Spanish Harlemites made an instant adjustment (some of them did and some of them didn't) but because Jim Vaus's philosophy is one of practical application. "We're not afraid to impose discipline," he says, "but discipline has to be imposed with love."

Basically, this is the creed of Big Jim Vaus. Everyone has to submit to authority. But the greatest authority is Christ. "I am convinced," he says, "that Christ wants control of your being and your life, and that you have to give yourself to Him wholly and completely. There is no other way to do God's work."

JOHNNY SPENCE

A Golf Pro's Symbol of Sunday

WEBSTER'S DICTIONARY defines the word "resurrection" as a state of rising from the dead. There is no word in Webster's for the state of rising from the *almost* dead—unless the word "miracle" covers it. Maybe miracle *is* the word for Johnny Spence. The man lay dying in the psychopathic ward of a hospital in Columbia, South Carolina; he knew it and wanted to die. His body lay shackled to the bed in a room with bars on the window and bars on the door. The six-foot, two-inch body had shrunk to 124 pounds. His official hospital description read: "blind in one eye, an alcoholic, a drug addict, indigent, an attempted suicide."

"Why a guy like that should go to the trouble of *attempting* suicide is beyond me. All he had to do was sit and wait—and not for long either, from the look of him," a nurse on the psychiatric ward said to the doctor.

The doctor nodded. "True enough, but from what I can see in his record, he's been attempting suicide ever since he was seventeen years old. That's a long time ago, but it's been a long suicide—and a slow one."

"Is there anything we can do for him—or *ought* to do for him?" she asked.

The doctor shrugged helplessly. "The book says 'glucose intravenously.' We'll try that, but I say we'd better get his family out here and call for the chaplain. I don't see him lasting through the night."

Johnny Spence would be the first to corroborate the doctor's diagnosis. It had been a long suicide and a slow one, and it had started when he was seventeen years old, more than thirty-five years before.

"I can even pinpoint the day," he remembers. "It was a Sunday. I was only seventeen, but I was the golf pro at the Ridge-wood Country Club in my home town, Columbia, South Carolina. . . . Pretty young for a pro, wasn't it?" he asks proudly. "But I was good in those days."

You survey quickly the tall, graceful body, the powerful hands that had swung golf clubs thousands of times on countless courses around the country, at the weather-beaten face that reflects a thousand fairways, and you recognize the athlete he once was. Even the pockmarks on his face and the leathery wrinkles (from sun and suffering) and the signs of tooth corrosion not quite camouflaged by the flashing big-toothed smile, fail to detract from the portrait. After more than fifty years of hard living, Spence still retains the sharp features of a ruggedly handsome man, not unlike those of the classic American Indian: straight nose, high cheekbones, strong chin.

"But what about that Sunday," one asks, "thirty-five years ago, when it all began?"

"It didn't seem like anything much then," he sighs. "I was a kid with a dream job—on my way to fame and fortune. What difference did it make if I had to work on Sundays?"

Then he explains what working on Sunday meant in his life. He had come from a religious family; especially on his mother's side. She was—and is—a devout Lutheran and today, at eighty-one, the only living charter member of the Church of the Ascension. His father, superintendent of the Columbia Railway Gas and Electric Company, in charge of streetcars, could take religion or leave it. He left it when Johnny Spence was fourteen; he left Johnny's mother too.

His father's divorce from the family huddled the remaining members into a solid unit that stood fast against the world. Johnny Spence and his two brothers tried to make up for what their father had taken away from them. They worked hard to provide the necessities of their living and they prayed hard to make up for their mother's loss.

Their mother told them never to put their church second. Were they ever to downgrade God, she warned, the devil would surely come into—and take over—their lives.

"We listened to her," Johnny Spence says. "We went to church regularly. We prayed regularly. We were good Christian boys." He stopped and smiled ruefully. "Guess it doesn't take much to be a 'good Christian' if you don't have to sacrifice anything for it. But I did, and I had to make a choice."

He remembers the day of choice. It was Sunday, and the seventeen-year-old golf pro did what he always did. He observed the Sabbath. He went to church, he prayed and he worked not. For Johnny Spence, the Ridgewood Country Club was off limits on the Lord's Day.

"That's the most ridiculous thing I ever heard of in my life, Johnny." The Ridgewood Club president was making an effort to keep his temper under wraps.

"I'm sorry, sir. It's just the way I been brought up. My mom is a mighty religious woman."

"I have nothing against your mom being religious, Johnny. But she isn't in the golf business. *You* are."

Then the president went on to explain the golf business to Johnny Spence. Golf, to golfers, wasn't work. It was play. The members worked during the week. Their playtime was Sunday, and they wanted—*expected*—the club's golf pro to be around.

"And don't forget, Johnny," he added significantly, "the Governor of South Carolina and the Mayor of Columbia are members here; not to mention all the business and industrial leaders in town." He paused. "And where do you think they are on a Sunday? I'll tell you where they are. They're right here, playing the game. More than that, they're trying to *improve* their game. . . . Look, son, you may go to church every Sunday and pray for them to be graduated from the duffer class, but that wouldn't do any good. Besides, they don't want it that way. They want you here, where you can show them how to grip the club, improve their swing, stop their slicing and give them pointers on putting. You can't do that for them sitting five miles away in a church pew, reading the Lord's Prayer."

Young Spence shook his head, bewildered. "Sir, I don't know what to tell you."

"You don't have to tell me anything, Johnny, because I'm going to tell you. And I'm telling you because you're still a kid and I'm making allowances. . . . You're the best damn golfer in the state. But more than that, you're a born teacher. You know what makes you good and you have the ability to show people what would make them good. Besides, they like you and listen to you. . . . That's a hell of a lot going for a seventeen-year-old kid. Men twice your age would sell their souls for your opportunities. But I'm not asking you to sell your soul. I'm not asking you to give up your religion. If you want to go to church, fine. I go there myself. But make it an early-morning service and spend the rest of the day out here. . . . That's not asking too much, is it?"

Johnny Spence had thought about it for a minute. "You make it sound reasonable enough, sir. I wish I could make my mom see it that way."

The older man sighed. "That's up to you, Johnny. You got a great future here. I'd hate like blazes to see you blow it. But I'll tell you this: If you can't work on Sundays, I can't use you. I'll have to hire someone else."

Johnny Spence went into a phone booth and called his mother. He told her what had happened. He wasn't surprised when she said he was putting golf before God.

"You can't do it, son. You just can't do it. All you'll have in the end is misery and suffering."

He tried to explain. He told her that his job was paying for the house they lived in, the car they drove, the food they ate.

"We had this house and all those other things before you

became a golf pro, Johnny. Somehow we'll still have them. Now, you quit that job and come on home. God will provide."

First it was his father who had provided. Now he was providing. But would God provide? Besides, what about his love for the game? He couldn't see himself giving it up. It was his life. And what the president of the Ridgewood Club had said was gospel; golf was a Sunday game.

"Johnny! Johnny!" his mother called over the telephone. "Did you hear what I said?"

He heard but didn't answer. Instead, he lifted the receiver—it pressed down like a weight lifter's dumbbell—and dropped it on the hook. . . .

"That was the day," he says now, "when I not only hung up on my mother, I hung up on God. . . . From that day on, I was all golf—I ate it, slept it, lived with it. It was my whole life."

Others have done no differently, but golf didn't do to them what it did to Johnny Spence.

"It isn't the game alone," he reminds you. "There are ramifications to golf just as there are in any other game. Maybe 25 percent of the players enjoy the game for the sport of it. The other 75 percent sweeten it up a little with some betting on the side."

The Ridgewood Country Club catered to the rich and their tastes ran to some high-caloric "sweetening." The favorite wager was $1,000 Nassau, which added up to betting $1,000 on each nine holes and an extra $1,000 for the entire match. Before long, Johnny Spence was holding more money in his hands than his mind had previously been able to imagine. But there was more too: his local golfing fame blazed—especially after he beat out top PGA professionals in dramatic sudden-death playoffs—and opened up unexpected avenues for him. He wrote a golf column for a local paper. He took on the job of teaching an accredited golf course at the University of South Carolina. He even went on the radio, singing Irish songs to his thousands of admirers.

"Those were the days of the devil," Johnny Spence remembers. "Everything materially was going my way. I didn't even take time out to regret my mom's disapproval. I was living it up, high on the hog—making money, enjoying myself."

A good deal of Johnny Spence's enjoyment was coming now from his job at the university, where his forty-seven students were coeds. The university crowd was a jolly one; moreover, they were in his age group. Before he knew it, he was a regular at the college dances. And before he knew it too, he was dancing and drinking with the rest of them.

Without benefit of formal education, he was big man on the campus. Without assets of elegant family origins, he hobnobbed with bankers, politicians, professional men, and anybody who was anything in Columbia, South Carolina—especially if he took up golf. It was, for Johnny, the swift, short and easy way, and who could prove that there was impropriety in the method.

"Don't think I didn't have qualms about drinking at first," he tells you. "It wasn't only my religious past, it was my athletic future." He laughs. "But those girls could sure talk you out of both your past *and* your future."

Johnny Spence describes his year and a half at the Ridgewood Country Club as a "riotous time." In his published autobiography, *Golf Pro for God,* he wrote: "Now that I had learned about women, all of them seemed fair game. Now that I had learned about liquor, I was taking a postgraduate course in drinking."

For the first time in his young life, his all-consuming passion for golf was diluted by his all-consuming passions for women and whiskey. It didn't take long for him to become bored with his job at the club. He told himself that he was young, with a great thirst for living, and that he wanted to see something of the world. So he patted his pocketful of money, resigned from the club and set out for greener pastures.

His first stop was Hartsville, South Carolina. There he took on the job of putting the finishing touches to a brand-new golf course that was the best in the area. He stayed on for a while, playing and teaching—giving as many as twelve lessons a day—while he drank and caroused to his heart's content. As it did in his home town, the job began to pall. It took a back seat to his other pleasures, which weren't as rewarding as they had been in Columbia. . . . So, fortifying himself with a wingdinger of a spree, Johnny Spence left Hartsville and took off for the sun and fun of Miami.

Here he didn't make the mistake of mixing business with pleasure. Miami, for Johnny Spence, was *all* fun. Next stop on the hegira of joy was New York. In the big town Johnny did what he had done elsewhere; he bought the wingding nights of revelry, paying with hard cash and intermittent hangovers.

At one point, he pulled himself together enough to go back to his home state and try to straighten himself out. He got a job at the Florence Country Club; it didn't last long. Again it was the same story: while the fun blossomed, the work faded, and on his twentieth birthday he awakened, sick and fuzzy-headed, in a fleabag hotel on the Bowery in New York City.

"It scared me, I tell you," he says, shuddering a little. "There I was at the bottom of the barrel and I was barely out of my teens. I had made it a lot faster than all the broken bodies and minds around me. They were all older than I was but I could match any of them in the shakes-and-shivers department. . . . Luckily, I had enough money left to pay my way back home. And that's what I wanted to do—go home to my mother."

There was no thought in his mind to find another job as a golf pro. He was incapable of holding a toothbrush in his hand, much less a number-two iron. But he wanted to stay on. He hoped, somehow, to get hold of himself and crawl his way back to where he had been. So he took a job (the first one that came along) as a theater doorman. He didn't mind the work, but the rest of Columbia did. They remembered Johnny Spence when he had been burning up the fairways, the boy wonder of the links, who played with the Governor and the Mayor, gambling and winning the $1,000 Nassaus. And almost overnight, a moviehouse flunky in a monkey suit.

Some of the citizens of Columbia looked the other way when they passed the theater. Others stopped to ask him what had happened. A very few shook his hand and told him they were sorry. All of them—no matter what they did or how they did it—accomplished one thing: they drove him back to drink. He couldn't stand their patronizing, their sympathy or their studied avoidance of him. In fits of moroseness, he wondered if the movie house had hired him as a local freak, for publicity purposes.

"Maybe I'm being unkind," he says reflectively. "Maybe it wasn't them at all. Maybe it was just me. Maybe I was just using them as an excuse for hitting the bottle. And I hit it, I tell you. I couldn't wait to get through at the job to get to my booze. I staggered home every night; just managing to make it."

He was in that "after hours" condition one night when he happened to meet his father on the street.

"Johnny!" the elder Spence said, putting his arm around him. "It's good to see you. How are you, boy?"

The boy jerked away, cursed the man and started to walk away.

"Son, I can help you," his father called after him. "If you want a job, I have one for you. . . . Remember that. I have a job for you."

Although he went to sleep that night cursing his father, Johnny awoke the next morning remembering his words.

"What do you think, Ma?" he asked his mother at the breakfast table.

"He's your father, Johnny. You loved him once. I'm sure he still loves you. Whatever happened between him and me has nothing to do with you. Don't judge him. Go to him."

He took his mother's advice and Mr. Spence got Johnny a job as a bus dispatcher and then as a bus driver.

"I guess he put me on as a driver because he knew I couldn't drink and drive a bus at the same time. And he was right too. I did cut down. I did my drinking after my regular run."

It was while Johnny was driving his bus that he met the girl who would become his wife. He describes her as a "beautiful girl; fine and educated too." She wouldn't have anything to do with him at first. His reputation had preceded him. He courted her for three years before they became engaged. He didn't stop drinking. He just stopped drinking when they were together.

"We loved each other but she was afraid," he says, "and who could blame her? I was a little afraid too. She was in my blood, but alcohol—gallons of it—was in my blood too. I knew I'd have to give up one or the other. I couldn't have them both. So I swore off the stuff and we got married."

For a while he kept the pledge, and he and his wife worked hard (she was a medical technician) to build a life for themselves. They saved money and made plans. Johnny wanted to get back into golf again. His wife recognized it as an encouraging sign and she agreed. They bought a tract of land—185 acres of it—on a hill overlooking the city and built a country club. It was a struggle all the way; not only to save what money they could but to arrange for loans to finance their dream.

In September of '41, they opened the Riverside Country Club. Three months later their membership totaled 338. But then World War II began and, little by little, the membership dwindled away. The younger golfers either enlisted or were drafted. The older ones—working on the home front—didn't have the time—or the inclination—for play, or the gas-rationing coupons to get to the club. A year later Johnny Spence and his wife were hanging on by their teeth. The Riverside Country Club was down to a membership of ten.

"We may as well face it, Johnny," his wife said, "we can't go on any longer. We haven't taken in enough this month to mow the grass."

"Don't I know it!"

"It can only get worse, Johnny."

He laughed. "No, honey. It can only get better."

She looked at him. "Have you lost your mind?"

"Not yet. I'm working on something."

The "something" was a deal with the U.S. Government. It involved the huge base which the Air Force had built outside of town. And Johnny was working out a plan with some Columbia, South Carolina, politicians to convert his country club into an officers' club. All he needed was a federal license and he would have a swinging operation going for him. It would mean an open bar and slot machines, both of which were barred to a civilian club.

"I got the federal license all right," he tells you, "and for a while I thought I was the luckiest guy in the world. Making money hand over fist. Couldn't even keep track of it. . . . But looking back at it now, I don't know if I was lucky after all. Those fly boys sure loved their booze. The club was swimming in it. I bought cases of half-pint liquors for forty dollars and I sold them for ninety. Money was no object if they could get what they wanted. And they were generous kids too. Always buying me a drink and I was always drinking it. . . . Never had it so good. I wasn't only enjoying my liquor; I was making money while I was enjoying it."

He thinks that if it weren't for the draft—which finally caught up with him—he would have (at the rate he was going) died of alcohol poisoning at about the same time that he would have become a millionaire.

It wasn't much of a war for Johnny Spence. Before he was even formally inducted and took his oath of allegiance, he was sent on to Pinehurst to represent Fort Bragg in a military golf tournament that lasted five days. On his return to "duty," he was immediately assigned to the base athletic program with such baseball stars as Ernie White of the St. Louis Cardinals, Van Lingle Mungo of the Brooklyn Dodgers and Jake Early of the Washington Senators. Johnny Spence's tour of duty consisted of golf instruction to the officers on the base.

He sums up his World War II experiences in one pithy sentence: "I played a lot, drank a lot, and came out a corporal."

In 1946 Spence thought he could take up his clubs again and match his skill against the best of the professionals on a national golf tour. It was a winter tournament that started on the West Coast and moved across the country into the South. The experience proved devastating.

Day after day a professional golf tour is charged with ten-

sion. One good chip or one bad putt can make the difference between a large purse or nominal also-ran money. The nights become pockets of relaxation. The big winners have learned the art
of unwinding while protecting their bodies. But many a talented
performer in the professional golfing ranks has succumbed to the
quick-shot technique of relaxation—living it up while drinking it
down—and with disastrous results. The tension and the temptation demanded too much of Spence's low tolerance of discipline.
Always he had possessed the liquid-powerful grooved swing. Off
the tee and on the long fairway shots he could smash with the
best of them. But tournaments are won around the green. The
demands in this area call for the delicate touch of accuracy and
finesse that springs from band-iron nerves and meticulous control. When Spence awakened after a night of revelry with hangover and shaky hands, he surveyed his plight and returned again
to the bottle. The round robin of excess rapidly crumpled him
into a quivering wreck. Golf, his obsession, became the mocking
tyrant, the measured proof of whiskey's victory over him.

"It was enough to make me take the pledge, and I did. For
six weeks I didn't go near the stuff. I substituted a regimen of
good living for my drinking. I'd take long hikes before breakfast,
eat good food, exercise and get plenty of rest. The results were
miraculous. I felt like a new man. I figured if this was what whiskey was doing to me, I could do without it. I honestly thought I
could." He stopped and shook his head sadly. "It was a fine piece
of irony the way I slipped and fell on my face."

Spence's fall from sobriety was irony with a wrench. At the
peak of his recovery, a friend asked him to attend a communion
service at a Lutheran church. What could be more innocent and
in keeping with his new life?

"That's what I thought too—until I drank that little cup of
wine the church used in its communion services. That did it. No
sooner had I downed the cup than I was off and running. The
taste of the stuff opened the gates of my thirst. After the services,
I made for the nearest restaurant. I ordered a bottle of wine. It
turned out to be wine from the presses of the Christian Brothers.

That made it kosher as far as I was concerned. I finished off the bottle and had another."

After that, Spence remembers little except that he went on a whirling binge. He went from town to town, from friend to friend; and wherever he went and whomever he was with, the story was always the same: drink and more drink. He doesn't know—to this day—how he got to Fayetteville, North Carolina, but that's where he ended up; in a hotel room where he stayed for three days and did nothing but drink. The binge culminated in his first attack of delirium tremens. He ranted like a wild man, destroyed furniture, screamed, rolled on the floor and banged his head against the walls. When the hotel manager tried to get near him, Spence threatened to kill him. Fortunately, the hotel was able to locate his wife.

"When I heard her voice at the door," he remembers, "I knew I was home again. I let her in. She took my hand as though I were a little boy, led me out to the car and drove me home. After I was put to bed, she called the family doctor. The next thing I knew, I had been committed to a private sanatorium in Aiken. I couldn't believe it. My wife wouldn't do this to me. They said she didn't want to but it was the family doctor's recommendation. When I saw the bars at the window and the guard at the door, I really went nuts."

The sanatorium doctor said, "If you'll just relax for a minute, I have some medicine here that'll settle you down and make you feel better."

It was Johnny Spence's introduction to drugs. The doctor gave him a slug of paraldehyde. In three seconds he was out cold. When he came to, he was strapped to the bed and there was a guard standing over him. After that they gave him a shock treatment and, after the shock treatment, he was kept on a steady diet of paraldehyde.

The drug is a classic weapon against alcoholism. A powerful hypnotic, it quiets the most ravished of nerves and separates the patient from the agonizing hallucinations of delirium tremens; the pink elephants depart the ceiling for the zoo; the patient finally gets to sleep and awakens into sobriety. For Spence, the drug worked as expected. In a few days he was up and around; so much so that he was free to move about and submit to physical therapy. This last consisted of raking leaves on the sanatorium grounds.

"I saw it as an opportunity to escape from that nuthouse," he says. "And one day I did. Armed with a sizable bottle of paraldehyde, I raked my leaves all the way up to the gate and the guard who stood there. When his back was turned, I clobbered him with the bottle and knocked him out. Then I was on my way home again."

The terror of the experience scared Spence into another personal campaign to win control over his weakness. Again he returned to a spartan physical life: exercise, good food, rest. And again it worked.

"I didn't know how long it would work because I had to have something more to keep me busy. Fortunately, it came along. A golf-equipment company asked me to represent them in seven Eastern states, with headquarters in Washington. It was an answer to a prayer. I grabbed it. The job was a snap for me: visit the country clubs and convince the pros to push our equipment. It was a new and good life."

One weekend, months later, the job took him to Pittsburgh and the Dapper Dan tournament. There he met an old friend, Kirby Higbe, who was pitching for the Pittsburgh Pirates. Johnny went to a Saturday game and watched his friend get bombed by the New York Giants. The tempestuous curve-baller headed for a bar to anesthetize the pain of the defeat. Higbe wanted company, and Johnny couldn't refuse.

"It was the same old story. I got plastered. It seemed as though I used any excuse to crawl back into the bottle. If it wasn't my frustrations, it was the other guy's. But the result was the same."

Johnny's wife didn't understand it. Nondrinkers never do.

"Why can't you be a social drinker?" she asked. "Why can't

you wait until five o'clock, have a drink or two before dinner and let it go at that?"

"OK. That's what I'll do. No more drinking until five."

It served as a weak out. For a while he kept to the time schedule—no drinking before five—but then he began to rationalize. He told himself it was always five o'clock somewhere in the world (London, Rome, Istanbul) so if he wanted a drink at noon his time he always managed to find a part of the world where it was five o'clock. On his more conscientious days, he stuck to his bargain, but only after he set his watch ahead to make up for the lost hours.

"Aside from that," he says, "I had a million other excuses. If my wife was a little late meeting me or if my baggage was delayed on a flight, that's all I needed to head for the nearest bar."

Somehow, Spence was able to keep a degree of surface control; the people he worked for were never fully aware of his problem. Exposure could mean the loss of a rich income and a return to renewed frustration. The incentive to stay dry once sent him searching out Alcoholics Anonymous.

"Once I was on a beer binge for twenty straight days. Drank so much of the stuff I almost drowned inside. Thought about AA but was too soaked to do anything about it. Another time was at a golfing banquet in Grand Rapids. I was sitting at a table with Lloyd Mangrum and Lawson Little. The waiter put a bottle of whiskey on the table. I ran like a thief and this time called AA. Didn't work. There was something about their mumbo jumbo that put me off."

By this time Johnny Spence was in business for himself. Sammy Snead and Mangrum had backed him in a real money-making venture: an open-air golf shop, set up in a tent or a trailer, which became a fixture at all the professional tournaments. He traveled a lot, sold quantities of equipment and drank as though the country were on the verge of prohibition. His temporary salvation was the interval between tournaments when he went home to Columbia and dried out at a rest home. It cost two hundred dollars a week plus "extras," but it was worth it because the rest-home people were kind and considerate. They didn't deprive him of his whiskey; just tapered him off.

"Sounds pretty good, doesn't it?" he asks with a wry smile. "Drink all you want and then take a two-week rest cure that guarantees you against the shakes and the DTs."

The neat little drink-and-dry routine, however, began functioning in reverse. It drew him into the fool's-paradise illusion that he could live it up to any degree because the rest home would take up the pressure of the aftereffects. Before long he was drinking more than he was drying. Again an insistent sense of morbid reality made him know it. This time he went to a legitimate rest home, where the cure was complete abstinence—cold turkey. But such was the anomalous character of the man that on his way to the cure he got himself roaring drunk. More than that, he even made provision for the uncertain future: he locked six bottles of Scotch in his car trunk and drove with comfort to his "cure."

"Only a hundred-percent, honest-to-goodness drunk can explain that," he tells you. "But a hundred-percent, honest-to-goodness drunk never bothers to explain."

Spence lingered at the legitimate rest home as long as the cache in the trunk of his car held out. "When that went, I went. I walked out of the place, went into town and had a couple of beers."

After his steady diet of hard whiskey, beer was an anemic substitute.

"Here, friend, why don't you try one of these things?" The man beside him offered a bottle of pills. "They're yellow jackets —Nembutal. Just drop one in your beer. It won't float, but *you* will."

The yellow jackets had quite a sting to them. Two of them with two beers and Johnny Spence was floating, all right, but he wasn't walking so good. He barely made it back to the rest home, where he discovered that the trip back wasn't worth the effort. The doctors took one look at him and sent him packing.

"It isn't everyone who can flunk out of a rest home." Johnny

Spence winks at you with his one good eye. "But when it came to alcohol, I was a dropout every time. For the rest of the year and the rest of the tour, I deserted the pledge for good reasons and bad. I'd get drunk if I had a bad day or I'd get drunk if I had a good day and cause for celebration. One Sunday when I was playing golf instead of going to church, I made a hole-in-one. Of course, I had to celebrate. So what did I do? I got drunk—that's what I did."

This was the year 1950. His earnings averaged almost $5,000 a week. His drinking continued heavy. Even his hangovers were impressive and, when he brought them home, his wife suffered cruelly.

"The woman's a saint." His voice reflects the affection and respect he has for her. "I did things to Dottie that a man wouldn't do to a dog without embarrassment. I guess I was too stoned to be embarrassed." He pauses—to find the words and the courage to express them. "I used to bring women home with me—my female drinking companions and admirers. I'd say they were nurses. Brought them home to pull me through the night. Then I'd take them into the bedroom and lock the door. Dottie knew. But she suffered through it."

Spence was suffering too. The hangover guilt for the misery he was inflicting on his wife and his mother tortured him. And accompanying it was the terror that he would drink away all the new business success and skid again into the horror of the New York Bowery.

"I didn't know what to do, where to turn. I was afraid of a legitimate rest home. There was no out in those places. They either cured you or killed you. I decided to go back to my original rest home. They knew me there. But this time I would do it *my* way."

He told the head nurse, "No liquor. If I plead for it, beg for it or grovel for it—no liquor, please. . . . I have to dry myself out once and for all; for good."

He was in bad shape but he was right about their kindness. The nurse gave him a shot of Pentothal and he was out.

For the first time, Spence went through a rest-home experience without a drop of liquor. He was high but he was dry. After his initial shot of Pentothal, the nurse put him on Nembutal. A teaspoon of the stuff—or a pill—in a glass of water was like four fingers of booze, straight. He felt ten feet tall and raring to go. Here, he thought, was the answer. The Nembutal had all the joys of drink without any of the penalties—no hangover, no whiskey breath, no DTs. He felt as though he were standing on the edge of a bright new world.

"First thing I did was get me to a doctor who understood my problem. He gave me a fistful of prescriptions. . . . Sure, he gave me the usual advice about taking the Nembutal sparingly. But you know me. I was never one to hold back on a good thing."

The Nembutal held Johnny Spence together through spring and summer and the professional tournaments that piled up relentlessly. But in holding him together, it also held on to him with a tightening grip. His dependence on the drug grew to such proportions that if he was in Chicago and running low on prescriptions, he'd fly back home to the doctor who'd replenish his supply. But all this time, no liquor—not one drop of it.

He thought he could go on like this forever, but "forever" ended at a country club in Atlanta. It was an important meeting with the sponsor of his tours. Everything had to go right, so he loaded himself with Nembutal and sat down to a business luncheon. He also sat down to a slug of whiskey that was supposed to toast the success of the upcoming year.

"Under the circumstances," he tells you, "I couldn't refuse. And that's where I fell off the wagon with a bang. That shot with the drugs was dynamite. I passed out."

It was hours later when Johnny Spence came to. What he came to was a blur of consciousness, but he got into his car with the sodden conviction that he had to get home, that his wife was waiting for him. Behind the wheel of his brand-new car, he took to the road. Somehow, he managed to find the route that he wanted. It was Highway 215, but Highway 215 wouldn't hold still for him; he weaved all over the road. Maybe if he stopped and had a couple of beers, the highway and he might come to a mutual understanding.

After the beers, he tried it again. If anything, it was worse. Now there was absolutely no rapport between his car and Highway 215. When he zigged, Highway 215 zagged.

"The battle ended when a tractor-trailer came between us. I took a curve on the wrong side of the road and there it was looming up ahead of me—a steel monster. The crash was terrific. My car was demolished. The truck suffered $8,000 worth of damages. My damages were one lung gone—pierced by a piece of my steering wheel—one broken hand, five teeth sheared away and, as they say in the accident reports, 'multiple cuts and bruises.' "

After a month of stitching and patching, what was left of the body of Johnny Spence was released from the hospital. His appearance was such that old friends didn't even recognize him. Nevertheless, he carried on. He doggedly joined the tournaments, taking himself wherever they took him. Now his medication was codeine to ease the pains of his accident. But codeine alone didn't help him. So he went back to whiskey and Nembutal. By balancing one against the other in careful dosages, he managed to maintain an acceptable façade that didn't give him away until he attended the golf celebrities tournament in Washington, D.C., where Sam Snead was the star. There he fell apart. Somehow he couldn't maintain his balance of whiskey and drugs. He knew he couldn't carry on. So he left his wife to make excuses for him while he planed back to Columbia and his favorite rest home.

It was the same old Johnny Spence who returned to his "last resort" but the nurse was a new one and she came equipped with a new trick for the patient. This was Demerol, a synthetically produced narcotic. One shot and Johnny Spence was a giant who owned the world.

"Never felt so good in my life," he remembers. "Never had such a good time in my life."

It turned out that the new nurse was not only a good one but a "nice" one. Before long, Johnny Spence's room took on the aspect of a Roman orgy. There were wine, woman, song—and Dem erol. The first week was the greatest. After that—and for some unknown reason—the edge seemed to be wearing off. He couldn't understand it. He was getting his regular shots of Demerol—and he knew the caliber of the drug—but the results weren't the same. Now he was only half a giant and he owned only half the world. Through the euphoria, he noticed that his nurse never drank with him yet *she* seemed to be walking on air, possessed that half of the world he had lost.

"I didn't know what it was. In my condition, I could only think sideways. Even so, I was determined to find out why. I was determined to keep my eyes open."

A day later, the nurse came into the room holding a needle loaded with Demerol. Spence feigned sleep. Through half-closed lids, he watched her as she lifted his arm, swabbed it and started to plunge the contents of the ampule into his veins. Peering intently and apprehensively into her patient's face, she stopped halfway, removed the needle, inserted it into her thigh, through her uniform, and drained it into her own veins.

"I reared up in bed and grabbed her wrist. . . . 'Goddamn it! What are you doing, girl? That's *my* Demerol. I pay for it through the nose. You're stealing it from me.' "

"Please, Johnny . . . I need it as much as you. Don't turn me in."

How could he turn her in? He felt sorry for her. She was hooked just as he was. But she couldn't afford it the way he could.

The pathetic irony of Spence's situation was that his skill at earning money made the purchase of expensive addictions uncomplicated. There was always whiskey and, should the rest home prescribe cold turkey, he could always rely on the "wine cellar" in the car trunk. And if he craved drugs, a well-paid doctor would accommodate with a prescription. The thought of becoming addicted never assaulted his conscious awareness.

"When you're going through the miseries the way I was, you'll take anything to get relief," he explains. "Also, I really believed I could kick any habit. All I had to do was *want* to kick it badly enough."

From time to time, Spence proved it to himself. During the 1954 West Coast tour, he got off the Demerol. But the agony of withdrawal made its demands; he returned to whiskey. For the rest of the tour, which wound up in Augusta with the Masters tournament, he stayed with whiskey. Occasionally he would go to Nembutal or Tuinal (a capsule sedative) when the pressures mounted but he tried not to mix drugs and drink. He succeeded until the Masters, when his old friend Sam Snead won a close one-stroke victory over Ben Hogan. Johnny had a bundle of money riding on Snead so, of course, he had to celebrate. Double whiskeys all around . . . and around . . . and around. Poured over a base of Nembutal, the result was a king-size blackout that lasted for three days. This scared him enough to try another rest home. He really meant to do it this time—all the way; wrap up all his addictions in one neat bundle and bury them for good.

"That's the way it was with me all the time. My particular hell was paved with the best intentions. Naturally, I washed out of the place. It was a legitimate cold-turkey rest home, and I just couldn't face up to it. So it was back on the treadmill again. Drugs and drink; even went back to the syringe and Demerol. Drugs were the only thing that kept me going; those and my visits—between tours—to my favorite rest home, where the curing was easy."

One such visit Johnny Spence will never forget. Among his patient-colleagues was a powerfully built man who sported a nasty disposition and a set of filed fingernails that extended a half-inch beyond the fingers. The impression he gave was that of a giant with ten razor blades hooked to his hands.

"About a dozen of us there," he writes in his autobiography, "were high on morphine. We were floating around the recreation room, hooting and hollering and just enjoying ourselves, when somebody began to play the piano and several of us began to sing. . . . I happened to be standing close to the man, so in sheer camaraderie I threw my arm around his shoulder. It was as if I had triggered a bomb. He whirled around and backhanded me with the flat edge of his left hand and I felt as if I had been blackjacked. Then that shovel-size right hand flashed into my face like an iron claw, and indescribable pain exploded in my head as his knifelike nails gouged into my right eye.

"He plucked out my eye as if it were a grape."

Johnny put his hands to his face. He could feel the blood pouring from the socket and the eye dangling on his cheek. He roared with rage and pain and went after the man with a metal ash stand. The giant crashed through a French window and fled onto the rest-home grounds. In agonizing fury, Spence chased him. But before he could take ten steps on the grass, he collapsed and passed out.

A rawboned German nurse picked him up and carried him back to the room and placed him on the floor. He struggled to rise.

"You'd better lie still, honey, or you'll bleed to death." She ordered another nurse to get a paraldehyde needle and a doctor.

"The doctor took one look at me and went to work. Kneeling beside me on the floor, he placed my dangling eye back into its socket. Then he sewed up my lower lid, which had been torn wide open. Only then was I moved. First to a bed and then to a hospital, where I stayed for thirteen weeks."

The thirteen weeks were not wasted ones for Johnny Spence. The doctors worked hard to keep him from losing his eye and they succeeded. But it was only a partial success. He had his eye but it would be sightless forever. He spent those ninety-one days planning and scheming for his revenge on his assailant. He decided, finally, that he would blow him to bits with a double-barreled shotgun. But the madman simply vanished. That frustration, aggravated by the constant pain from his slowly healing eye, drove him back to drugs and whiskey.

"When I was able to take to the tournament trail again, I was in terrible shape. I wore dark glasses to hide my blind eye and, when someone asked, I told them I had been hit by a golf ball. . . . It's hard to believe," he reflects with wonderment, "that while I was experiencing a slow, personal, physical death, my professional life was booming. Despite the thousands of dollars I was throwing away on my addictions, I was able to amass a small financial empire. I owned an office building in Columbia, South Carolina, sizable real-estate holdings in Florida, two trailers worth twelve thousand dollars and three automobiles. There wouldn't have been any limit to the fruits of my labor if only I had been able to keep laboring."

More and more, he spent less and less time tending to his business. His desperation drove him from one rest home to another. In one such haven he spent more than $11,000, plus "extras." In several others he was strictly a straitjacket patient. And his final debasement occurred in a Philadelphia clinic, where, in order to reduce the violence of his delirium tremens, the doctors had to inject a half-pint of whiskey into his rectum.

At an extreme point in an alcoholic's career, his stomach lining becomes so ravaged from the excess of alcohol that more liquor, the only quick relief for the patient's craving, will swiftly be vomited out. Alcohol injected directly into the colon is absorbed quickly into the bloodstream. It achieves the effect while avoiding the insult to the stomach lining. This is bitter knowledge to veteran alcoholics and Spence has since explained that long later, he himself administered the treatment to a drunk in the throes of the DTs who screamed for help.

When he emerged from this degrading experience, Spence knew again that he had "had it." In a desperate effort to salvage something, he trained his nephew to take over the coast-to-coast golf tournaments. His sponsors wouldn't have it; it was either Spence or no one. So it became no one. Swiftly followed a toboggan slide. First he sold one of his cars, then his trailers and, finally, his properties. All of them went fast but all of them couldn't keep pace with his expensive addictions.

"To get a 'fix' once, I sold a $7,000 trailer for $750." The $750 kept him in a rest home for five days. When it was gone, he was gone, as far as the authorities were concerned. He called his wife to pick him up and take him home. To tide him over he had a bottle of paraldehyde stashed away in his bedroom. One jolt of the stuff and he passed into oblivion.

Sometime during that night, he woke from his stupor, wanting another slug of paraldehyde. But he couldn't find the bottle. He couldn't remember where he had put it. First he tore apart his room, looking for it. Then he ran through the house, from room to room, upsetting furniture, tearing open drawers and cupboards, upending the rugs, pulling apart the beds.

"I was a raging madman. My wife, my mother, my brother were there. They couldn't believe what they saw. And they couldn't believe it when I turned on them, screaming that they had hidden my drug from me. They swore they knew nothing about it. And I didn't believe them. I swore I'd kill them if they didn't come up with it fast."

He grabbed a shotgun and brandished it in front of their staring eyes. "Find that bottle," he screamed, "or everybody in the house gets it."

Suddenly everybody started running. His mother bolted through the door and scurried outside. Johnny stumbled after her in the yard, yelling at her to show herself so that he could kill her. When he failed to find her, he charged into the house, found his wife and held the shotgun on her.

"I swear, I'll kill you if you don't come through with that bottle," he roared.

Then the police arrived. A neighbor had called them to investigate the bloodcurdling yells. They sized up the situation in a glance. One of them stepped behind him and hacked him senseless with a judo shot on the back of the neck.

To doctors who observed Spence's addiction, the raging dependence on drugs and the reactions to the particular drugs he selected seem medically anomalous. Drugs such as Nembutal and Tuinal are hypnotics for most people, inducing drowsiness and torpor. Demerol, a basic pain killer, gives some a lift from agony but does not generally produce a hallucinatory trance of well-being. Paraldehyde is usually not an addictive drug; it produces rest and a dulled nervous state. Spence never actually utilized heroin, which does produce the "high" effect with melodramatic suddenness. He had the money to get it but somehow, without overwhelming conscious effort, he never searched it out. Possibly the most reasoned explanation lies in Spence's psychic makeup. Behind the carefree, drawling charm, there churned a burning, tense nervous structure. Liquor, basically a depressant, served efficiently as a calming agent. Its aftereffects, certainly beyond modest use, produce symptoms which for a golfer can be nothing short of calamitous. The hands shake, the body quivers, coordination flees with the hangover—and good golf is impossible. The more one drinks, the more one needs; it is a tournament of defeat. Though Spence sensed it, his proud country-boy spirit refused to accept it. The next step in the psychic, raging battle was the ally, drugs. They did hold off the need for whiskey. They did induce calm and they did it quickly. The paraldehyde episode was less attributable to the addictive effect of the drug than to Spence's screaming fear that he would be left naked without it and reduced to craven prostration before the brute in the bottle.

After the almost homicidal episode in his house, he came to in the ward of the city hospital. The doctors kept him there, again believing they could cure him of his drug addiction.

"It was a good try," he remembers, "but it was like a whisper in a tornado. They didn't understand the shape I was in. They couldn't appreciate my constant searing pain, my never-ending desperation. I stood it as long as I could and then, one day, I put on my clothes and walked away from them."

He went home and his mother tried to help. "Son," she pleaded, her eyes flooding with tears, "please come back to God."

He told her not to worry, that he'd make it his own way. Immediately he sold one of his two remaining cars. The money was enough to keep him on drugs long enough to contact a friend, who gave him the job of running an open-air golf shop at White Sulphur Springs for the Sam Snead Festival. The job paid him $500.

"I guess it was too much for me. I celebrated with a combination of Demerol and whiskey. I had reached the point where I couldn't take them separately. I took them together—a tablet in a glass of booze—and that did it for me again."

To this day, he doesn't remember how he made it back to his favorite rest home. But it wasn't the same rest home. A new group had bought it and his $500 kept him there for only a week. No money—no drugs, no treatment. . . . He staggered into the outside world cold broke, with a two-day growth of beard and a bad case of the shakes. He went to friends to borrow money but, by now, they knew his plight and he couldn't raise a dollar. He wandered around town until he stumbled upon an old acquaintance—a long-time alcoholic, squatting in a doorway nursing a pint of whiskey, which he willingly shared with Johnny.

When the pint was gone, Johnny Spence achieved the perception that sometimes comes to the addict in an inexplicable flash of awareness. He realized he couldn't make it any more. He was on the Bowery, the skid row of Columbia, South Carolina; and this time there would be no recovery.

"But there was one thing I wanted to do—more than anything in the world. Before I gave up my ghost I wanted to see the country club I used to own."

Somehow he managed to find his way to the house of a friend. He pleaded, begged for a ride to the setting of his old glories. The man agreed despite misgivings about Spence's condition.

When they reached the club, the man stopped the car. "Well, there it is, Johnny. You wanted to see it and here it is.

"Well, what do you say, Johnny? Shall we go back?"

"I'm not going back, buddy." Johnny Spence opened the door of the car. "See the river over there? I'm walking into it. I'm going to drown myself, once and for all."

He stepped out of the car, fell flat on his face and rolled into the mud. The man bundled him back into the car and took him to the nearest government hospital. He regained consciousness in a room with bars on the windows and doors, and his six-foot-two emaciated frame strapped to a bed—with a guard, a nurse and a doctor administering glucose. They called the chaplain, an old, retired preacher.

"When the chaplain came, I tried to get rid of him. I told

him I didn't want to be prayed over. I told him I wasn't worth saving, not to dirty his britches on the likes of me. But he insisted and I didn't have the strength to argue."

The chaplain fell to his knees beside the bed, grasped Johnny Spence's hand and began to pray. At first the words seemed meaningless but then the chaplain said something that roused Johnny's mind: "God, this man thinks that he is bad. He isn't bad. *I* am bad, Father. *I* am a sinner. And if you would save me, Father, I know you will save him. . . . Father, I want to thank you in Jesus' name."

The chaplain stood up and tightened his grip on Johnny's hand. "You're going to be all right, son. All you have to do is look to God. Try to pray and I'll pray for you."

He lay there for a long time after the chaplain was gone, thinking of the man's words, saying them over and over to himself.

"Mr. Spence . . ." It was the guard. He had been in the room all the time. "Mr. Spence, what the chaplain said was right. You should turn to God. You should pray, and I'm going to help you."

He removed the shackles from Johnny's hands. "Here, let me help you up."

Johnny shook him off. "No, thank you. I've got to do this myself."

He didn't know where his strength came from but he struggled erect, put his feet to the floor and stumbled to the barred window. Clutching the casement for support, he looked out into the night and he saw the yellow street lights. He looked up into the sky and he saw the twinkling stars. It was so long since he had noticed them and they were so beautiful.

He turned to the guard. "Boy," he said, "I've never prayed out loud before in my life but I'm going to do it tonight. I'm going to do it now."

"You go right ahead, Mr. Spence."

There, at the barred windows, Johnny Spence bowed his head and prayed. He told God that he knew he was going to die.

He recited his sins, one by one. He renounced his addictions, and he asked for only one thing: that the Lord cleanse him enough so that he could hold himself together for a last visit from his mother. She was the one who had stood by him. She was the one who had never stopped praying for him. She was the one whose heart he had broken so many times. And now he wanted her to see him when he wasn't in a fit of delirium tremens, when he wasn't shaking, when he wasn't crying. . . . If God would only do this for him, he would be His servant forever.

"After I prayed, I stumbled back to bed. The nurse came in. She had some medicine in her hand. I guess she figured I was so far gone, it didn't matter if I had another shot of dope to make it easier for me. I shook my head and told her I didn't want it."

The nurse looked at him in amazement. Here was a man who had in turn pleaded, begged, screamed, demanded relief from his agonies. And now that she held his bottle of relief in her hand, willing to give it to him, he was refusing. More, disdaining it.

"What goes with you, Spence? I don't understand it," she said.

"I'm not sure I know myself. All I know is that I don't want any of that stuff—ever again." He looked up at her. "Tell me something, nurse. Are you a Christian?"

She nodded. "I like to think that I am."

"Then would you pray for me—please?"

Without a word, she dropped to her knees beside his bed and began to pray.

"I suffered that night. All the hounds of hell were chasing through my broken body. The pangs of withdrawal—of cold turkey—were like fangs gnawing away at my insides. I had gone through this before but, somehow, this time it was different. The suffering was horrible but it was also purgative. It was as though I were undergoing a treatment, not a trial. . . . And I took no medication—no dope, no whiskey. . . . After what seemed like ages, I managed to fall asleep."

For weeks afterward, Spence kept fighting, but this time he felt that he wasn't fighting alone. He was fighting with God's help. Even so, it wasn't easy. The road back was slow and painful. The insistent shakes prevented him from holding a glass of water to his lips; he lapped at it like a dog. Even the Bible had to be held for him. But slowly he was converting each day into a rung on his ladder of salvation.

"One day the hospital chaplain asked me if I would do him a special favor. He wanted me to go to the chapel that evening to a planned prayer meeting. He knew I would have difficulty making my way there alone but he thought the effort would be worth it because the meeting was going to be conducted by an old friend of mine, someone who was deeply interested in my welfare. I couldn't imagine who it was."

"It's Emory Harper, Johnny, an old golf pupil of yours, a man who has been deeply influenced by Billy Graham. Do you remember him?"

Of course he remembered Emory Harper. He had won the state golf championship one year and used to be one of the crowd. But then he had attended a Billy Graham revival, and everybody soured on him—wouldn't touch a drink, wouldn't gamble, wouldn't even smoke. Johnny had pegged him as a hopeless religious fanatic, and did his best to humiliate him whenever he had the chance. Spence told the chaplain that he must be mistaken; no Christian could be *that* Christian after what he had done to him. But the chaplain insisted.

The chaplain provided a wheelchair, and Johnny started his laborious journey. The effort was too much; along the way he fainted, fell out of the wheelchair and gashed his face against a rock. When he came to, he was covered with blood. Through the pain he could hear the singing in the chapel: "Just as I am, without one plea, but that thy blood was shed for me, O Lamb of God, I come."

The words were inspiring enough for Johnny Spence to pull himself up from the ground, desert the wheelchair and make his way—hanging on to tree and bush—to the open door of the hospital chapel. There he faltered. His strength had been drained away. But there he could both see and hear Emory Harper.

"Fellows," Emory Harper was saying, "if there are any of you who are suffering from fear and anxiety, or if you have anything wrong with you that you haven't been able to cure, turn it over to God. Let Jesus Christ take your burden. . . . If you want to receive Him as your Savior, raise your hands."

Johnny Spence raised his hand and, like a flash, Emory Harper was striding down the aisle to the door and confronting him.

"Aren't you Johnny Spence?" he asked.

"Yes, I am."

"Your hand is raised, isn't it?"

"Yes. It's raised."

Harper looked at him. "Do you mean business? God means business, but what about *you?*"

"I mean it more than anything in the world."

With that, Emory Harper took him in his arms and held him close. "Thank you, God. Thank you for Johnny Spence. I've been praying for him for more than eight years, and you have answered my prayers."

After the meeting, Harper escorted Spence back to his room. They talked for hours.

"I wanted to know how a man I had done so much wrong to could pray for me."

"When God came into my life, I accepted him," Harper explained. "Christ transformed my mind. The bad things passed away. You must remember, Johnny, that Christ is not only our loving Savior, he is our living Savior."

"Four days after this meeting, I was discharged from the hospital. I wasn't completely well, but I was as close to being well as I had ever been in a long time. No one has to tell me about miracles. I am a living, breathing miracle."

In the weeks that followed, Spence slowly made his way—

step by step, day by day—back to health. Now, even though he was penniless, he felt that he had to show his gratitude to God by helping others find their way to Him.

"The first thing I thought of was that old chapel on the hospital grounds, where Emory Harper had helped me find my way to Jesus Christ. 'That hospital ought to have a new chapel,' I told myself, and I knew just how to get one. I went to Sam Snead and Mike Souchak, two of the great golfers in the world, and asked them to play an exhibition match for the building fund. They agreed without a moment's hesitation and without a penny's worth of compensation."

The Snead-Souchak exhibition was a huge financial success that went on long after the match ended. Money for the new chapel kept rolling in from golf fans and well-wishers all over the country.

"Fourteen weeks, to the day, after I made my conversion to Christ I attended the Billy Graham crusade in Charlotte. Billy spoke to the great crowd and told them about me. He said I was his spiritual godchild. When he concluded his remarks, he asked me to say a few words. I was scared stiff. I didn't know what to say. Somehow, I managed to make my way to the pulpit and, somehow, the words formed in my mind and—as the Bible promised—came forth from my mouth. . . . I told my story to the thousands gathered there; from sin to salvation. . . . I must have made a good impression because after the meeting, Billy's associate evangelist, Grady Wilson, asked me to repeat it for a television audience."

Following the Charlotte crusade and his television testament, Johnny Spence received dozens of invitations to tell his story to private groups and organizations. Sometimes his expenses were paid and he received a small honorarium. Sometimes just his expenses. . . . And many times nothing; even though he might be speaking to five hundred people who had paid $2.50 for the privilege of hearing him.

"I was being exploited by some so-called Christians who left me high and dry hundreds of miles from home. It was a devil-testing time for me but somehow I managed to hang on to my faith."

The wrenching setbacks of cavalier treatment, disillusion-ment with others and personal discomfiture waved before him as red flags of temptation. Always there existed outside sources of sudden comfort. This time, Spence could turn away from the problems and find surcease in a large faith. On some occasions he would sit long hours with Graham talking and reflecting. The help he received spiritually and sometimes materially from Graham in nonpublicized loans brought him closer to the evangelist as a friend and even closer to the way of life he espoused so vigor-ously.

Obviously, the road back for Spence, beyond his devotion to his rekindled faith, led to the golf links. And as his friends began to see a new Spence, stronger than twenty years earlier, even more adroit with the driver and wedge, new offers to teach and to man-age golf courses started to seep in. Spence would have wanted nothing more. But a nagging doubt remained. Golf was *too* good to him. The symbol of his downfall was pegged on the matter of giving up the Lord's Day for the links. Not for others—but only for Spence, who still sees this as his own besmirched escutcheon. And to give in would mean to abandon his refound beliefs in favor of his private symbol of Christian rejection. One rich man offered to build a golf club around him. The condition queered the deal—be there on Sunday. Spence had to refuse and he swears that he simply cannot consider breaking the pledge.

Essentially he is a gentle, drawling, easily warmed man who simply cannot find it within himself to judge others. He is grimly aware of how torturous it was for Johnny Spence to judge him-self. And since he has come this far, he is equipped to address himself primarily to his own spiritual needs. He knows what *he* must or must not do. As for others, he is willing to tell his har-rowing story to them without sparing the cruel details. If it helps them make a better life, Johnny Spence is revitalized by the won-derment that a man who fell so low could help others rise again.

What he defeated was not the raw fact of dope addiction or alcoholism alone. The former was the by-product of the latter. First he was a drunk who tried to ward it off with drugs. But always he vibrated with a hot, highly strung interior, never entirely satisfied with himself, driven and driving toward an unattainable end. What the whiskey, the material success and the dope failed to deliver, a comprehending surrender to faith provided. He is, today, not driven, not overdemanding of his skills and not beset by corrosive ambition. His faith leaves him content, as affable within himself as he had always been on the surface toward others. In short, he is a happy man.

He speaks for pittances or for nothing. He ekes out a living in joyous contentment, never looking back at the old affluence invidiously. He is happy in God's world—and every day of his life he will keep thanking God for giving him another chance.

JEAN DILLARD

The Creative Role of God in Art

TOO INFREQUENTLY is Christianity associated with joy. Religion, to many people, conjures up images of solemn followers enshrouded in a uniform of sackcloth and ashes, burdened by fear and trembling. The idea carries with it a language of clichés—"born again," "saved," "converted," "salvation," "blood of the lamb," and a score of other familiar and oft-repeated phrases. On the surface, this is what the idea of a certain language of Christianity has brought to people; more important is the query revolving around the idea of what people have brought to Christianity.

The question was asked by Jean Dillard, a Christian who is also an artist with seven "one-man" exhibits to her credit. Mrs. Dillard is a *born-again, saved, converted* Christian who has made her *decision for Christ* but eschews the language because it smacks of cliché and she doesn't believe that Christianity should ever suffer stereotype.

"I know that thousands of Christians whose lives have been changed through conversion speak a limited, warmed-over jargon because they are at a loss to express themselves in any other way. But I also know that it's this very same language usage that scares others away. To the nonbeliever, it smacks of a brand of Bible-beating, hell-fire revivalism, alien to our times and to the fresh winds of ecumenism that are revitalizing our century."

A sophisticated, vivacious intellectual, with the handsome good looks, lithe figure and good cheer of a cultivated hostess, Mrs. Dillard draws the source of such gifts less from the finishing school than from the deep font of her faith. "I always enjoyed human contact," she explains.

"But the real dimension came with my renewed contact with God. Once that happens, you love people, naturally, without condition or restriction. It really makes a difference."

This total round-the-clock awareness of God—its words and deeds—involves little formal religiosity. At one time she felt a sense of guilt because her paintings and sketches (almost a thousand of them) were not religiously oriented; no pictures of Calvary, The Last Supper or depictions of the loaves and the fishes.

She spoke about this once—almost apologetically—to Leighton Ford, Billy Graham's brother-in-law, who is an admirer of her work. Ford laughed. He reminded her that every painting, every work of art, was in a sense a religious painting, a religious work of art because the subject matter—whether it be a bird, a flower, a landscape, a figure, a still life—was a reflection of God's work, just as she herself was a reflection of the Lord's will.

"Was it always this way with me," she wondered, "before I admitted Christ as my need and my dependence?"

Jean Dillard was born in Rock Hill, South Carolina, a doctor's daughter, a child of a solid Southern family with a good Christian background that predetermined a good life for this striking auburn-haired girl who possessed an abundance of physical and intellectual energy. Like most Southern girls with a similar heritage, she made her way to maturity through the right avenues: proper upbringing, active church participation and good schooling. She attended Winthrop College in Rock Hill—a liberal arts institution—from which she was graduated with a double major in Art and English. After graduating, she worked for a year in New York City as a dress designer and as a model for the famous John Robert Powers Agency.

In 1937 Jean married E. S. Dillard, the scion of a huge

paper-box-manufacturing empire. In Charlotte, North Carolina, where the couple lived, life was not only good, it was luxurious: a big house, cars, a boat, even a private plane. Jean Dillard was a socially integrated young matron. At the country club she played golf and tennis, swam and water-skied. She was active in church and community-welfare affairs. She read avidly, especially in the fields of philosophy and religion. Rabbi Joshua Liebman's "Peace of Mind" made a vivid impression on her. Billy Graham's books and newspaper columns were a source of renewing inspiration.

"Looking back at those years now," she says, her voice rich with the accents of the South, "I sometimes wonder how I managed to do everything I did. Most busy people complain about the days not being long enough. For me the days were always long enough and I used every minute of them."

Jean was thinking of her other activities: her sewing, her needlework, her clothes-designing for the children when they started coming along (there are three of them—two girls and a boy), her pottery work, her painting (murals for the nursery and the children's rooms), even bricklaying. The bricklaying was a patio she built on her hands and knees, in the back of their house, a ten-month, three-thousand-brick project, laid out in artistic designs. A touch of irony crowned the completion of the task; when she had finished, the Dillards moved from Charlotte to Lynchburg, Virginia.

"Naturally," she laughs, "we couldn't move my precious patio with us. But I really didn't care. You see, the house was sold to Queens College, a religiously oriented Presbyterian school, for use as a girl's dormitory and I was sure the students would enjoy it almost as much as I enjoyed building it."

The explanation of why the wife of an extremely wealthy businessman, whose position was imposing enough to elect him a director of the National Association of Manufacturers and to be named as one of the foremost young business presidents of the year, should become a spare-time bricklayer, designer and family dressmaker, rests with the feverishly creative energy built into her psyche. When her children grew up and demanded less personal attention, Jean began painting seriously as an additive to her whirlwind schedule of local activities. In recognition of her well-rounded accomplishments, the city of Charlotte named her "Woman of the Year."

"I suppose it was because of my background and the full life I enjoyed that the suddenness of my marital situation hit me with such devastating force."

She describes the marriage and its cruel dissolution with surprising absence of rancor or recrimination. Rather, there is thoughtful evaluation of a relationship turned blighted for the two people involved. Before the first break came, she suffered awareness that areas in the marriage lay wanting. Her love for her husband was deep and unyielding. But she was beginning to doubt parallel feelings on his part. And then, one morning, she woke to find herself and the children deserted. He walked out suddenly with neither warning nor explanation.

The predictable reaction to such a situation is quite naturally shock. Jean felt the tremors and, accompanying them, the assorted pangs first of fear, then of guilt, then of swelling waves of anger. Together they boiled into an inner stew of bewilderment. Her marriage had never been easy. Her reaction to her husband's personality, one rent by inarticulate anxieties, was to accept or explain it with a loyal wife's forbearance for her mate's business problems or inner personal ones over which he possessed only limited control. Certainly, none of these irritations presaged abandonment.

That night in March, 1951, she was desolate. She went to a small guest room, fell to her knees, wept and prayed and talked aloud with God. "I've been a good wife, a good mother; I've done everything I know to make myself what my husband and children wanted of me. But I know this couldn't happen if I was doing right. I want you to take over, Lord. With all my heart I accept Christ as my Savior. From now on, You are first in my life. Help me out of this despair."

It was a solitary conversion—no crowds, no counselors, no preacher.

"People always ask me if some sudden change came over my life when I let God take over," she says, "some miracle—at least some junior-size revelation. It wasn't anything like that at all. It was merely that somehow things started falling into place for me."

In the empty days and weeks that followed, Jean Dillard kept trying to fathom the cruel facts in the light of her new understanding. Never could she summon from within her the certitude of enough rage or righteousness to level the lance of blame entirely upon her husband.

She sought help from her close friend and minister, the respected Reverend James A. Jones, now president of the Union Theological Seminary in Richmond, Virginia. He listened patiently to her saga of agony and broke silence when in protestation Jean exclaimed that always she had placed her husband and her family ahead of all in her life.

"Do you know what you're saying?" he asked.

Jean shook her head, puzzled. "What do you mean, 'Do you know what you're saying?' Of course I know what I'm saying."

"No you don't, Jean. You only think you do. What you're really admitting is that you're an atheist."

Jean was indignant. "How can you say such a thing, Dr. Jones? I've been a good Christian all my life; an active church member. I believe in God. Must I start proving that now?"

"Of course, you believe in God, Jean. But you admit that He hasn't been *first* in your life. Your husband has been first. Then your children. For you—and for many Christians—God is relegated to the space beyond. Think on that. Perhaps it will help you."

Jean left the church and walked back to her husbandless home. She walked with the challenging words of her minister ringing in her ears. Now she recalled that Billy Graham had repeated the ideas over and over again in his books, his newspaper columns, on the radio and television and in his crusades. In the past the ideas had titillated her intellect. Never had they pierced the armor of her feelings with such depth.

The concept kept nagging. Strangely, it reverted to New Testament basics; Jesus had commanded his disciples to follow his vanguard before their fathers and mothers. The subtlety of the injunction often bewilders the literal-minded in a conventional society which teaches that obedience to mother and father and loyalty to family is paramount. Ostensibly, to place any of them in one's loyalties other than paramount would seem as though they were relegated to a purgatory of second best. Though the truth of this is proved by the language and its sequential logic, what eludes the well-meaning believer is the subtlety of the injunction. The undercurrent of that command is the concession on the part of one believer that nothing supersedes the essence of faith; that once the omnipotence of God is accepted, then all of these creatures must of necessity be subject to His primacy. The metaphysical concept of the essence of God would not presuppose that one could be half loyal to another of his creatures. Quite the contrary. It carried with it the power of God's love, the tuning in to His purpose, the humbling of self before the spiritual world of faith and the relegation of the secular world to its proper place— an area of Divine creation subject to God's will. To place that secular world in an orbit around self and then have God revolve around it as a satellite would be to impose falsely the order of man's orbit in the spiritual cosmos. To replace those bodies to their proper orbit would demand an understanding of the connection between God and Man.

On her way home, and in the cheerless rooms of the grand house, Jean pondered the symbolism of Dr. Jones's cryptic words. And slowly the meanings enlarged, the logic hardened and her consciousness fell into a current of spiritual persuasion.

As one who has counseled with potential and eventual converts, Jean Dillard knows from close hand the diverse ways by which a spiritual rebirth takes place. To some it is an explosive revelation, to others a gradual awakening; to some it is achieved via persuasive pulpitry, to others from silent reflection and reading. Only the end result is common to all. For herself, an alert, intellectually oriented woman, the subtle, cerebral implication of

Dr. Jones's challenge and the supplementary power of Graham's no-nonsense thunderings on the subject brought her psychically and spiritually to the shoreline of these metaphysical waters. Then, with prayer born of sincerity and conviction and of a desire to place herself beneath the force of God and in his dependence, she became a reborn Christian. The failure of the marriage and its concomitant pain shook her confidence in herself alone and in the sanctity of secular institutions. But the essence of this conversion was not, simply stated, an exchange of a cozy religion for a marriage failure. The latter helped Jean Dillard to recognize the fallibility of all humans and their institutions—and the inviolability of God's institution. And finally, that without spiritual dependence she traveled half armed in an insecure world.

Many friends, some who had prayed for her, now helped her achieve the transition. She went with them to prayer meetings, visited their houses, packed up and took her children to Montreat, North Carolina, where she attended an Annual Bible Conference and thus started emerging from a life that had been a tinted shell.

In 1957 she had returned to Queens College to take special courses, some in art. At previous times she had studied painting, had painted sporadically and sometimes well. Now her oils and watercolors seemed to take on new dimension. While she had previously departmentalized herself into Jean Dillard, wife, mother, painter, social worker, now she was just one woman, whole and complete, with all the facets of her being fusing into a core of purposeful activity.

It was during this period that she again queried herself about the absence of an obvious religious symbol in her work. The explanation surpassed, in her mind, the one Leighton Ford had enunciated. Ford had not explained content in terms of the subjective artist. Now, with her conversion, the answer was crystal clear. Her new conception of Christ was not the parochial one of agony and suffering. These reflected a small part of His being. To her, Christ was basically radiant; not the pathetic figure so often portrayed. An anemic Christ indicated an anemic Christianity. For Jean Dillard this was vexing and she refused to accept it.

Since her image of Christianity reflected a total positive view of life, she painted what she saw and felt in those terms. For the subject matter of her paintings, therefore, she employed the aesthetic fiber of her environment, infused with her spiritual attitudes about it.

Another truth which emerged from her new belief and her work was that she did not feel like a creator. She was a recorder, bringing the essence of inner truth to her easel. Thus she painted, inspired, spontaneous and free, always capable, at perplexing turns in her work, of feeling the security of dependence on strength that was never refused.

Seven months after Edwin Dillard left his wife, he returned and asked for a divorce. It was a painful meeting. He talked about the legalities: custody of the children, the properties, alimony. Jean talked only of the human relationship: the children, herself, the life they had built together.

In the end, he suddenly blurted, "I don't want to talk any more about divorce. I want to come home again."

It was more than all right with his wife. They decided to keep their reconciliation quiet until the following Sunday. Then they and the children would go to church and Charlotte would know that the Dillards were together again.

"When Eddie and I walked arm and arm into the church on Thanksgiving Day, 1951," Jean remembers, "there wasn't a dry eye in the house. It was an unforgettable day."

For the Dillards, life, at least on the surface, returned to the ordered, secure existence prior to the separation. But, for Jean, the new arrangement was buttressed by an added element. This time, come what may, she knew that she would never resuffer such loneliness as before; the inner companion was her inner consort with a vital faith. It gave her strength and a sense of certainty and permanence. Many times she remembered the Annual Bible Conference in Montreat and the experience of reaffirming her faith when she heard Billy Graham speak. She continually marveled at the certainty of his belief and the confidence of his convictions.

That year Billy Graham was not entirely a popular figure at

the Conference. A few ministers, representing all the Protestant faiths, reacted with disdain to his homespun homiletics and did little to mask their attitudes. Billy Graham knew their feelings, yet never struck back in defense. But as though each minister were his closest colleague he offered his own positive attitude toward evangelism. "When you talk over people's heads," he said, "it only proves one thing. You don't know how to aim." For her the simple statement transcended advice from pulpit to pulpiteer. It suggested the universal approachability of God's message, available to all, powerful because of its simple truths, less ecclesiastical than pragmatic. The admonition possibly did more for her than for the ministers. As a nonpreaching evangelist, she has never lost confidence in it and has never failed to marvel at its effectiveness in reaching people.

In the summer of 1960, after applying herself to work and study with several nationally recognized art instructors, Jean Dillard joined a painting tour to Europe. There were fourteen artists in all, under the direction of W. J. S. Cox, director of the New England School of Art in Boston. The group traveled to Switzerland, Italy, Austria and Germany, painting all along the way. Jean's output was prodigious. She boarded the *Queen Mary* on the return trip with no fewer than sixty watercolors painted in six weeks. The return trip to the States sparked her first—however informal—one-man show. Dozens of friends on board insisted on seeing her work. A couple who occupied the largest quarters offered the use of their suite for the showing. The guests applauded her efforts and, for the first time, she experienced the exhilaration of recognition as a professional.

It was only the beginning. In the three years that followed, Jean had five formal one-man shows. The first was at the Lynchburg Art Center in Lynchburg, Virginia. There followed shows at the Mint Museum of Art in Charlotte, North Carolina; the Children's Nature Museum in Rock Hill, South Carolina; the Hickory Museum of Art in Hickory, South Carolina; the Altavista Library Exhibit in Altavista, Virginia; and, capping them all, a well-reviewed New York show at the York Gallery in 1966.

The critics warmed her ears: "She has challenged an area of art often riddled with triteness and met this challenge with freshness, excitement and originality. . . . The artist has worked with a continuous variety of line and color as a skilled choreographer would compose and create with movements of the dance. . . . Jean Dillard is more than a technician. She has a temperament that reacts to subject matter; its mood and its fleeting atmosphere. Her brush is an extension of her personality. . . . The results are a stunning exhibition."

Jean Dillard loves the applause but reacts to it somewhat uniquely. She says little about "God-given" talents. "I don't really feel as though I'm creating. The beauty is there. It's all around us. What I'm doing is re-expressing it, reframing it, portraying it as I see and feel it, the way it was given to me. Every act, every word is a *sharing*. Each of us is an evangelist in his own way. All of us—whether we realize it or not—are involved in other people's lives. It's an awesome thing to contemplate. If we do it on our own—denying God's help—we're nothing more than bullies playing God, inflicting our stubborn conclusions on people who may have entirely different ones. . . .

"I don't have all the answers," she admits. "As a matter of fact, I have very few of them. There is no such thing as the complete Christian. I think *striving* and becoming is the closest to an answer; moving in a direction in a two-step-forward, one-step-back way, trying to interpret a particular problem to a particular person with Jesus as a guide. Somewhere truth will find a common ground that resolves itself in a oneness with God. I do know that when man's will and God's will converge, good emerges."

In her striving to find the direction of God's will, Jean Dillard immerses her person in no mystical moonlighting or romantic yearnings after miracles.

She does not project the missionary obsessiveness so offensive to the assaulted nonbeliever. Though she eschews the spiritual detective work to uncover potential converts, many of the troubled ones seek her out. It was always this way with her. When she was a little girl, her family used to call her "Atlas" because she was always taking on responsibility for others' problems; projecting herself into their lives. People still come to her for help, attracted by her candid warmth. But today there's a difference. Jean no longer bends under the weight of her own or other people's problems. She knows that she and they have to depend on a larger power for help and strength. To her and to them God is the only answer. But it isn't just a matter of "Ask and you shall receive." It's ask, *do* and give. *Do* all you can to help yourself; *do* all you can to solve your problems. And if you give yourself over to the Lord, He will satisfy basic needs if not all desires.

If this sounds like an individual, perhaps maverick approach to God, Jean Dillard admits to the distinction. She rejects a wholesale type Christianity, made up of rehearsed troops chanting answers to commands. "In this infinite world with its billions of people, its countless flora and fauna, there are no beings, no two things—no leaf or snowflake—exactly alike. Even so-called identical twins have their differences; if nothing else, their fingerprints vary. God must have wanted individual faces and individual minds. Why should we try to maim divine will? I think this applies to Christianity. God loves each as an *individual* and each should bring the stamp of his personality to his faith."

Jean expresses these ideas vigorously, especially to young people's groups. In essence, she proclaims, there can be no inherited Christian faith. As an individual each person must declare his own witness to God. No intercessor can make the offering for him.

She recalls her reaction to Billy Graham's approach to young people at one of his Charlotte crusades. He set aside special nights for the teen-agers and the young adults, who came from all over the state to hear him. But his message to the young people was not entirely different from his messages to older people. Though he adjusted the vocabulary to accommodate the age levels, Graham stuck hard to the essence of the New Testament message. Though, as a counselor herself, she feared at times that its unyielding tone would scare them away, Jean learned that it was precisely the refusal to talk down to them that brought them back. Later on, Billy Graham explained it to her: Young people don't want a soft faith. In a frightened, unbelieving world, they want a challenge to believe.

These young people's meetings so impressed her that she was determined to learn more about the dynamics of the teen-age mentality in terms of their religious awareness. In 1959 she registered at the Graduate School of the Union Theological Seminary in New York for studies in adolescent psychology. Much of what she learned there confirmed Billy Graham's outlook. She also learned that teen-agers had to be given freedom to develop their own faith in their own way. This was a confirmation of her belief in the individual Christian.

For twelve years the Dillards' reconciliation worked. Then, as suddenly as before, Edwin Dillard left and sent his lawyer to ask for a divorce. She answered that as far as she was concerned, their marriage was irrevocable, she didn't believe in divorce. But her husband was adamant. After an interim of legal jousting, Dillard flew to Nevada, obtained a quick divorce and remarried.

"It wasn't as bad as the first time," she remembers. "Now I had inner resources. Although I was unhappy for myself and my children, I felt compassion for Eddie. I understood his problems. I wished I could have made it easier for him. . . . I felt no bitterness and no desire for recrimination. I take no credit for this reaction. I owe it to a higher power. I might have acted similarly if I were he. . . . It's awfully difficult to overcome a childhood of unhappiness and the pressures of his adult life."

During the legal proceedings, Jean tendered her resignation as Bible class teacher and as chairman of several church committees, explaining that a divorced woman should not hold such sensitive posts in the Christian community. The minister flatly refused and insisted that she stay on; nonetheless she temporarily withdrew.

Even so, people gravitated to her with their problems and their interests. Frequently at one of her art shows a stranger will approach to praise her work; more often than not the conversation will drift to life, its purpose and its problems. Before long the talk gets around to nature and then to the supernatural.

"Spontaneously," she says, "I find myself sharing the gospel —personally, informally. I can't avoid it because art is only an extension of God. It expresses my zest for living, my love for life and my kinship with Christ. In art, of course, technique is important but it's the reaction a painter has to his subject that takes precedence over technique. One doesn't have to be an astronomer to appreciate a sunset. All one needs is the unencumbered freedom to see, observe and react."

There is little difference in tone or expression when Jean Dillard's talk turns from art to religion or vice versa. It's as though the subjects were interchangeable. She employs an identical manner when she lectures on art or teaches a Bible class. Her tall, firm, undulating body moves gracefully on the platform, expressing a point with a turn of her head or a movement of her eloquent hands. There are variegated dimensions in life and in people, she tells an audience, just as there are in art. Jean is very familiar with these dimensions and she knows their potentials as well as their demands. The physical changes in her mode of living following her divorce, for example, illustrate the point. Her large and luxurious houses in Charlotte and Lynchburg, Virginia, with their gardens and patios, are light-years removed from her small modest home in Sarasota, Florida, and the ancient five-room walkup she now occupies on Manhattan's Third Avenue, where she lives most of the year. But there is never any harking back to the past, or any complaints about the present. Actually, the New York apartment is very attractive, furnished with the confident, free-wheeling taste of an artist; antiques blending with modern comfort and everywhere paintings and easels.

The flat—which also serves as Jean's studio—is, in itself, an illustration of her belief that God provides for one's needs. When she left for New York she had a hundred of her paintings and watercolors crated and shipped by freight. These were scheduled to arrive several weeks after she did. In the interim she was supposed to find a place to live, establish a studio and find an art gallery to accept her work.

New York being what it is—with its high rents and its small apartments—this turned out to be a more difficult accomplishment than she had thought. Fortunately, two fortuitous circumstances carried her along. One was an offer of an apartment by a friend who was leaving the city for several weeks. The other was a chance meeting with a fellow artist, who explained the procedure the galleries followed in commissioning one-man shows. The artist didn't just present himself with three or four samples of his original work; he first had color slides made of *all* his work for the gallery to evaluate.

"I was really such an innocent," Mrs. Dillard says. "A real hick from the sticks. But no one had to tell me twice. As soon as my paintings and watercolors arrived, I had them uncrated and hired a professional photographer to take color slides of every one of them, with no thought of how they would be shown, much less accepted. For a month I continued to paint and frame as though a show were a foregone conclusion."

The day before the friend in whose apartment she was living was to return to the city, the director of the fashionable York Gallery, on East 56th Street, looked at her color slides and said he was interested. "Interested" meant that he was impressed enough to justify a look at the originals.

"Are they available, Mrs. Dillard?" he wanted to know.

"Not today. But they will be whenever you say."

"How about tomorrow—late afternoon?"

Jean blanched and nodded. "Tomorrow afternoon. I'll call you in the morning and let you know where."

It was an opportunity she couldn't pass up but it was an opportunity she didn't know what to do with. The paintings and the watercolors were uncrated. But she didn't have a wall to her name to hang them on. She returned to her friend's apartment, wondering what to do. Then she did what by now comes naturally to her: she prayed.

Shortly after her arrival in New York, Jean had made friends with a couple who owned an art-supply shop where she purchased her supplies. Hardly had she finished the prayer when the couple came to deliver some paintings she had had framed, and she discussed her problem with them.

"Look, Mrs. Dillard," Mrs. Friedman said, "we like your work and we like you. We own the building and a few apartments above our store. One of them is vacant. It's five rooms—not large, mind you, but very nice rooms—light and airy. One of them in the back is a studio. And the wall space is terrific. How would you like to rent it?"

Jean could hardly believe this bit of luck and was even more delighted when the owner told her he was willing to let her live in the apartment rent free for the rest of the month and for the two following months. She had her paintings delivered the very same day. She spent most of the night and the next morning arranging and hanging her exhibit. When she was through, there was time to spare before the man from the York Gallery was due to arrive. She invited her landlady to see if she had done a good job. She was quite nervous.

The landlady went from room to room, looking at the paintings and watercolors with a professional eye.

"You don't have to be nervous, Mrs. Dillard. If the York man has any taste and judgment, you'll have your one-man show." She stopped and smiled. "Besides, everything is bound to be all right because my husband and I have been praying for you."

The shop owner-landlord and his wife turned out to be orthodox Jews.

It naturally pleases but doesn't necessarily surprise Jean Dillard that things worked out so well, although so unplanned. The constant awareness of her inner spiritual dependence permits her to move atop the world with a premonition of protectedness. It is faintly related to fatalism but is at once more. It is a faith based on optimism, on awareness that, for worse or better, she travels with a protective companion who guides with love, and somehow, fear and insecurity seldom succeed in corrupting the relationship.

Jean Dillard firmly believes that her acceptance of the person of Christ has helped her to think bigger and be bigger than she is. As a traditionally reared Southerner, she lived with the social postulate that whites and Negroes were not only different but that the latter unquestionably were to occupy a lower level in the social structure. A full commitment to her faith reveals that absurdity to her with specific certainty. "God," she says simply, "is color blind. That's the answer."

As a Christian, she resents the use of the word "Christian" as an adjective of goodness. She is convinced that our churches are populated by too many rigid so-called Christians who so smugly believe in their piety that they think they can manage their lives on their own.

"I can't say this often enough because this is the way I feel deep down inside of me: no one can manage alone. All of us must be dependent on a larger power. Any other judgment is pure egocentricity. And that is not Christianity."

Her approach to God is through prayer without ceasing. Formerly when she heard the wail of a fire siren or an ambulance she would pray that it was not for *her* house, *her* family, *her* friends. Today she prays for whomever the siren sounds. So habitual has this become, that once when she sat transfixed before the television screen watching a movie about people facing disaster, she automatically began praying for them.

A more personal example of the change that has taken place in her life is her experience with flying. When she was married to Edwin Dillard, who had a private plane at his disposal and insisted on using it, flying was a terrifying ordeal. She was certain she would end up as a burnt ember in a fiery crash. Today Jean Dillard flies whenever the distance warrants it. She no longer has a fear of death. "Few truly committed Christians fear death," she says. "The awareness of everlasting life serves as a counterbalance."

Now that her children are grown and two of them are married, Mrs. Dillard has ambitious plans for the future. She hopes to publish a book on Christianity as she sees it. One of the chapters will be titled "Did Jesus Lie?" and it will express her belief in the validity of the person of Christ. She will show how she came to understand and believe *what* He said He was and *who* He said He was.

"Oh, I'm going to write about a lot of things," she says with contagious enthusiasm, "but it's all going to be in simple, layman's language because I think that's what Christians need for the reaffirmation of their faith and what non-Christians need to be introduced to the faith.

"I intend to write about the 'teen-age stigma,' and the general misunderstanding of our Christian youth, who need a forceful challenge in their lives. I want to explain *my* witness to Christ because it's the only witness I really know and understand. Then I'm going to write about the false straitjackets of a false, hypocritical Christianity, and how to break out of them. I want people to know that if they claim to accept the Fatherhood of God, they must accept the Brotherhood of Man."

The ideas and words flow freely, and she has shared them for fifteen years on speaking engagements. She is eager to explode some of the myths that surround her faith: like the myth that spiritual matters should be approached for solution on an intellectual level; or the myth that a true Christian can experience the feeling of righteous indignation, which, she insists, is a contradiction for one who is supposed not to judge lest he be judged.

The bubbling vital energy of this creative woman never fails to awe her friends, who wonder how she does it.

"My energy merely reflects my assurance of God's love. There is no magic to it. After I turned my life over to God, I was rid of most tensions which are the burdens and encumbrances in all our lives. As a result, my own latent energies were released. Now there isn't anything I can't attempt. I have a direct connection with God. I depend on Him for help and guidance. It may sound like a contradiction, but any strength I have is based on dependence. I need God. I need Him very badly. Without Him, I'd be lost and I don't want to be lost again. Nobody really needs to be."

STUART HAMBLEN

"The Words Don't Match the Face"

EXCEPT FOR his clothes, the man on the platform of the Midwestern prison auditorium might have been one of them. His face was rugged with the hard-boned handsomeness of the outdoorsman, yet looked as though life had stomped it with hobnailed boots. It was lined, battered, highlighted with a mended nose, and the small areas of scar tissue revealed a history of combat. His frame was massive. His hamlike hands were studded with broken knuckles. His half-hour speech to the inmates, laced with the insistent twang of the country boy, held the attention of the men embittered by their lot, resentful of society and hardened to the preaching do-gooders who assaulted them regularly with unwanted, and to them, hypocritical intonings. This fellow they knew for his fame—or infamy. He was Stuart Hamblen, the hillbilly singer and composer from Hollywood, a roaring hell raiser who had lived it up to the hilt and then got religion.

He concluded swiftly, pausing for a moment, then said: "I want to tell you one thing and I want you to remember it. . . . You guys think no one loves you or cares about you. I know what it feels like because I was once behind bars too. This old roughneck cares about you. More important—*Christ* cares and loves you."

The trusty at the organ swung into "This Old House," followed by Hamblen's other big popular hymn, "It Is no Secret," and the big man slowly strode down the center aisle in his rolling gait to the door, where he waited for the men to start back to their cells. One by one he shook their hands and thanked them for listening.

At the prison office, the warden thanked him warmly. "The men enjoy you. Most of them don't go to religious services. But when you come around, they all flock out."

Hamblen smiled. "I don't think most people like being preached *at*, especially people in trouble like these men. Nothing riles me more than to hear someone talking down to people. I know about that from close hand. My daddy was a preacher, you know. I try to level with these guys. I tell them what happened to me and how religion changed my life. I guess they figure if it could fix up an old roughneck cowboy like me, it could work for anybody."

On the flight home to Los Angeles, Hamblen relaxed and reflected. It was like all the other trips in the past fifteen years; a million miles of them at his own expense to prisons, youth groups and church meetings all over the country. He remembered them all and most of the people he had sung to and talked with. A raw contrast from the trips in the old days, when he'd get drunk, charter a plane and be deposited far away to sober up. Half the time he would black out and suffer brutal hangovers, remembering almost nothing. Consciously it never occurred to him that he wasn't having a whooping good life.

All the conventional creature-comfort symbols of the modern world he possessed: women, race horses, fame and money. He brawled and belly-laughed his way through every day. Even the meeting and courtship of his wife reflected the whoop-and-holler attitude of the rough-hewn man of action who thumbed his nose in the face of convention.

He first saw her in Hollywood on the crosswalk of Sunset and Vine, "The prettiest gal I ever did see in my whole entire life." He spun around, admiring the compact figure as he trailed her.

"Look, honey," he said as he overtook her, "I'm not just an ordinary masher. I got serious intentions for you. You and me are going to get married."

He laughed off her threats to call the police. "That'll do you no good, honey. I know every cop in this town. Now why don't you be a little sociable and have a drink with me? You might get to know me and decide you love me too."

The unconventional courtship involved continual footstep-dogging and a visit to another suitor. It was strictly out of a 1930 gangster-film epic. The frightened young man, hardly believing what he heard, stared into the scowling face of the six-foot, two-inch giant who roared that he stay away from Susie or "get his skinny neck broken, get it?" The young man "got it." He never tested temptation and was never seen again.

Eventually the "crazy hillbilly" won out. He bought a wedding ring, and the Oklahoma-born girl—worn down by attrition—walked down the aisle with him.

"There are just two kinds of wives in this world," he explains, "the legal and the loyal. I'm lucky. Susie has stuck with me when almost any other woman would have hightailed it out of my life. She refused to believe I was hopelessly bad. You know something, she didn't even bat an eye when I told her we were going to rope wild horses in New Mexico for our honeymoon. . . . But then I guess I've always been lucky with women. . . ."

The first woman in his life, his mother, indulged his impetuosities no less. When his conduct and her impatience soared beyond the range of bearability, she would weep and blame herself. She neither scolded nor whipped him. He was a restless headstrong boy despite his early sickly and puny condition. That fact, added to the itinerant habits of the family, made regular schooling difficult and personal tutoring necessary. Mrs. Hamblen taught him so well to read and write and do sums, that when he finally was registered at a formal school, he began in the fourth grade.

Life with his father represented a rigid contrast. A revivalist hell-fire-and-damnation preacher in the tradition of the Methodist circuit rider, the Reverend Hamblen neither understood nor accepted easily his wife's pampering of the devilish youth. A short, bellow-lunged man, he inveighed restlessly at sinners from the Panhandle to the Gulf. The family was constantly on the move. They knew well all the little sun-baked Texas towns: Knott City, Hamlin, Abilene, Stanford, wherever the local revivalist committees would invite them. Little of the preaching admonitions wore off on Stuart. "I didn't understand—or maybe want to understand —all my father's devil preaching," he says. "All I did understand was that if you had bad thoughts you were guilty, and if you were guilty, sure as shootin' you were going to hell. I sure couldn't stop those 'bad' thoughts—fun, dancing, girls. So when Dad would say I was heading straight for hell, I figured I might just as well enjoy the ride."

When Stuart turned twelve, his father took a new notice of him, this time physical.

"You're lookin' pretty puny, boy. You're growin' up straight enough but you're not fillin' out and you're not toughenin' up. What you need is a year or two on a honest-to-goodness Texas ranch. How does that strike you, boy?"

Whether it struck him or not, the boy knew he wasn't going to have much say in the matter. But he consoled himself with the thought that if he were going to hell, he might better enjoy it on horseback.

The ranch to which he was exiled was the Reed Double Circle. It sat in the Texas Panhandle, where the summer winds parched the land and the winter gales froze it. At first he hated everything about it: the weather, the country, the cattle—even the men. They were a rough-and-tumble crew and they didn't make life easy for a tenderfoot. He had to learn how to ride and rope. Separately these chores weren't too much for him but when he tried to combine them he became convinced that the cowhands would kill him before they could toughen him up.

"They'd sit me on a horse, give me a rope, point out a real wild snortin' bronco and tell me to bring him in. That was all right with me but it didn't sit so good with the bronc. I'd ride after him, running him around in circles while he snorted and stomped somethin' awful. Finally, I'd wear him out enough to get in close and throw the rope. Sometimes I was lucky, and I tell you it was a thrill to see that lasso sail through the air and settle down around the bronc's neck. But it wasn't a thrill that lasted long. As soon as the bronc felt the rope, he pulled up short and jerked his head around. That jerk lifted me clear out of the saddle and sailed *me* through the air to land smack dab in a patch of mesquite. I tell you, after six months of that kind of treatment, I developed a hide that was all callus."

Besides educated calluses, he developed a shrewd appreciation of horses—how to rate them, break and train them and race them successfully against the mustangs of his cowpuncher colleagues. That talent eventually brought him material dividends never envisaged by his pious father, who sent him to the country for reasons of physical health alone. In later life the Johnny-come-lately cowpuncher was to earn a fortune racing his stable of thoroughbreds at such worldly outposts as California's Santa Anita racetrack.

Another bonus of the Reed Double Circle ranch period was the boy's new awareness of music. Singing frivolous songs had been taboo in the full-gospel environs of the Hamblens. If the spirit called, at determined periods of the week, one intoned musical hymns to God. To the youngster weaned on the solemnity of "Jesus Loves Me" and "That Old Wooden Cross," lighthearted tunes of the world sounded the sweet notes of joy and liberation and fun. But within Hamblen home borders, such frivolity represented profanation of sacred premises, and one either sang religion—or one didn't sing. Stuart, who loved to sing and has frequently said that he "hears an orchestra in his head" even though he knows no formal music, kept mostly silent.

On the ranch lands it was different. After work hours he would sit quietly in the bunkhouse listening to the cowboys as they sang and picked at their guitars—the sad lonely songs of sad lonely men. Soon he began singing along with them and, when he was alone, he would pick out his own accompaniment. Occasionally, the "orchestra in his head" would produce a melody. When he mustered up enough courage to sing it aloud, the men applauded. After a while he made up and sang more songs and got to learn how to appeal to his bucolic audiences. They always loved him. In every way he became accepted by the ranch hands. In town they relieved the monotony of their lives by drinking hard and finding their pleasures in quick bursts unhampered by pangs of conscience. The "devil" in him that his daddy had warned him about had taken over. But to the young cowboy it was one great roaring spree and the devil with it. He was having fun.

By now he had become a slick itinerant ranch hand who could pick up board and drinking money at different spreads as the mood struck him and supplement his pecuniary needs with irregular country-music renditions.

On occasional home visits he felt even more alien than before. The paternal disapproval was sterner than ever and harder to take. "So I'd go ramblin' again," he recalls. "Traveled all over Texas, singing around, drinking, living it up. Guy at a bar says something nasty to me, I'd put up my fists and say 'OK, buddy, let's waltz.' Once in a while, I'd hold still long enough to take a course or two at a college. Nothing serious though. Too itchy to hang around for long anywhere. When I made a few dollars, I'd sew them in my old clothes and move on. It was a crazy kind of life but I loved every bit of it."

Dallas turned into a significant way stop. At a local theater, he sang "The Johnstown Flood," brought down the house and won the hundred-dollar first prize. These were the days of the Great Depression, when a hundred dollars was a young fortune. With the big money, he struck out for Los Angeles, where he figured a real cowboy could pick up good money in radio.

He was nineteen years old and the year was 1930. The sprawling city made him feel like a stray dogie. He had come in by bus, rubbernecked around for a while and retreated to the bus-terminal bench to figure out what to do.

"Something troubling you, son?"

The questioner standing above him was a little guy, pasty-faced and oddly unwelcome even to the lonely country boy. Hamblen stood up abruptly, walked away mumbling, "No, thanks," and stopped at a crowded newsstand.

"I stood next to a little old lady who was picking through the pages of a magazine," Stuart remembers. "Next thing I knew, this sleazy character was sidling up on the other side of me. He squeezed my waist and whispered, 'I like you. Why don't we have a drink up at my place?' "

It was Hamblen's first experience with a homosexual. He spun around, smashed his fist into the pasty face, and sent the little man sprawling into the magazine rack.

The bus terminal erupted into bedlam. The little old lady lit into Hamblen with her handbag and her umbrella, screaming, "You dirty bully," as the crowds gathered.

Hamblen started running and didn't stop until he escaped. He had had it as far as that "crazy town" was concerned. Twenty-four hours after his arrival, he was back in Texas, still scratching his head over the weird episode.

In search of work, he lighted in Bell, Texas, where the Ford Motor Company had a plant. Feeling newly comfortable and at home again in Texas, he dressed himself up in style—cowboy style: red shirt, tight pants, boots, ten-gallon hat; even a .45 on his hip—and swaggered into a poolroom.

One of the players set his cue stick on the floor and looked him over carefully and insolently, taking in the costume and especially the gun.

"Looks like you're all primed to pull off a job," he said, grinning.

Hamblen grinned back. "I sure am. I'm primed to pull off a big one at the Ford plant."

In country jargon he was just trying to say that he was confident of getting work at the Ford plant. City jargon for "a job" meaning a holdup was another language to him. Before Hamblen could sink the five ball in an end pocket, the police arrived and swiftly backed him against the wall.

"You the punk who's going to pull off a job at the Ford plant?" one of the detectives asked.

"I sure hope to," the bewildered youngster replied.

Without another word, one of the detectives pinioned his arms. The other, with professional certitude, spread-eagled a hand over his face, pushing back the skin around his eyes, rendering him sightless. He then methodically smashed him in the face, then in the solar plexus, and when he doubled up, uppercut him straight again and again till his body was a bloody mess. Before he passed out, Hamblen grunted at his torturer and swore through a broken mouth, "I'll never forget your face, mister. I'll pay you back."

Then they dragged him off to jail and booked him on an open charge, a ploy designed to let the culprit cool his heels interminably. Hamblen sneaked a note to his father, who was then engaged in a crusade in another part of the state. Reverend Hamblen sent a friend, Bob Shuler, a great and respected evangelist, who vouched for the boy and got him sprung from the Bell bastille.

Now Hamblen decided to give Los Angeles another whirl. After Bell, Texas, even the "crazy" city seemed civilized.

This time he was determined to make a real stab at radio. He had read that the famed announcer Don Wilson was holding auditions for new talent at radio station KFI. He dressed himself up in a white celluloid collar, pegged pants, tooled boots and a flaming red shirt. The black eye he still sported from his fracas in Bell, Texas, completed his costume. Don Wilson and the other KFI people in the control room took one look at him and roared. When he started his nasal twang of "The Johnstown Flood," the song that had won him a hundred dollars in Dallas, they doubled over. It was one of their first real brushes with hillbilly singing.

In the middle of his song, Hamblen suddenly stopped. "If you-all don't think much of my singing, I'll quit right now," he said.

Don Wilson and the manager in the control room assured him that they were just enjoying him. To prove it they put him on the "Midnight Jamboree" to sing the song, insisting he dress the same way.

"They weren't foolin' me none," Hamblen says. "They figured I was a clown good for a bushel of laughs. That's about all."

Much to everyone's astonishment, the hillbilly drew two sacks of fan mail in three days and more kept rolling in. In retrospect, it should not have come as such a stunning upset. To begin with, Southern California, even in the thirties, was the home of expatriates from all over the country, many of them from the real country—the South, the Midwest and the Southwest. They had been reared on the singing tales of the lonely cowboy and his gal and the Great Roundup. In addition, no indigenous American art form has ever come close in popularity to that of the American cowboy—then as well as now. And last, there was the matter of the Hamblen style; the voice is deep and rich, the phrasing is authentically country and the boy loved the tunes, he believed the words and he succeeded in doing then what he has continued to do to this day—mainly projecting a vivid, original personality.

That performance launched one of the West Coast's most enduring show-business careers. It began with a fifteen-minute Saturday broadcast that paid him fifty dollars. Then Hamblen moved into high uninhibited gear. He put on a good show on and off the airwaves. His troupe was the forerunner of the Beverly Hillbillies. He dressed them in tattered clothes, armed them with ancient rifles and drove around town, whooping and hollering. Years later he graduated to more elaborate productions. He created the "Covered Wagon Jamboree" and "Stuart Hamblen's Lucky Starrs." By 1949, one local show earned him $1,000 a program.

"It was only pocket money compared to what I was making on my stable of horses," Hamblen says.

On one horse alone—El Lobo—which he picked up for $2,500, he made $400,000. From the slick sophistication of the tinsel city, Hamblen learned little and changed less. He brought his country experiences there, complete with ten-gallon hat, country songs and a good head for horseflesh, and Los Angeles re-warded the stranger lavishly.

As soon as the money started rolling in from radio, he started buying horses. He usually had a few thoroughbreds in his stable and he trained them personally, hovered over them, booked them on the track and kept winning.

The notorious gambler Mickey Cohen then discovered him. One day at the track, after pocketing a particularly fat purse at Santa Anita, he found the little mobster waiting for him at the parking lot.

"Hamblen," said Cohen, "I'm Mickey Cohen. I want to talk to you."

Hamblen brushed past him. "Nice knowing you," he said, and he got into his car, behind the wheel, as Cohen followed.

"Look, Mr. Mickey Cohen, I train horses and I race horses here, and it's against the rules of the California Racing Association for me to even say hello to a professional gambler. Like I said, it was nice knowing you."

Cohen laughed. "Skip the boy-scout stuff, Hamblen. I just wanted to ask you something."

"Like what?"

"Like giving me a good tip on a sure thing for tomorrow. I got $5,000 to put on one of your nag's noses. I'll make it worth your while."

"And suppose the nag's nose doesn't make it?"

Cohen shrugged. "In that case, I'll give you time to pay me back the money."

Hamblen reached inside the glove compartment, and in one swift motion yanked out a .45 revolver and pointed it at the gam-bler. "Look, Mr. Mickey Cohen, if you don't blow out of here, I'll blow your goddamn brains out. Is that clear?"

Cohen blanched and blinked; his stubbled jowls quivered perceptibly. He turned and wordlessly walked away. Hamblen never heard from him again.

The horses indirectly afforded Hamblen the opportunity to repay a debt of ten years' standing. He spotted an unforgettable face at the track. The detective who had beaten him in Bell, Texas, was now a guard at the racetrack. Hamblen walked up to him and smashed him to the ground with one punch. Then he picked him up and knocked him down again.

"I don't know how many times I punched him," he says. "All I remembered was how this guy had clobbered me blind."

He now smiles sheepishly as he describes the event. "I guess I wouldn't do that today. You know, being a Christian and all. But I'm not a turn-the-other-cheek kind of Christian. I don't understand that business of putting up with everything. That don't make sense to me. I like a Christian who stands up for what he believes in—in and out of religion."

Aside from his radio and horse-racing interests, Stuart Hamblen wrote songs, more than a thousand of them. Before his conversion, the songs were raucous hillbilly ditties—like "I Won't Go Hunting Jake But I'll Go Hunting Women."

"It wasn't till I found Christ that I began to write a different kind of song. 'This Old House' was one of them. I guess my biggest, as far as money goes. But the others haven't done bad either: 'Open Your Heart and Let the Sun Shine In,' 'It Is no Secret' and 'Oh, His Hands.' "

Hamblen's songs made his third fortune for him; the lasting one, because the royalties from them still keep rolling in now that radio and the horses are gone. One of the most profitable ones, "Oh, His Hands," he donated to Dr. Jonas Salk for his research activities. "In the old days," says Hamblen with a grin, "I'd have bought me another race horse."

It was those early flush bachelor days that started him on his skid to near disaster. The money poured in and Hamblen poured it out just as fast. He drank interminably, intermingling mealtime and bartime with such compulsiveness that most of his waking hours became involved in a wild nonstop ingestion. Increasingly, through the bleary stupor of the hangovers, the insistent truth of his condition lanced his consciousness with terror. He couldn't keep away from it. He would saunter into a bar half pretending to himself that he wanted to meet a friend. The sober side of

Hamblen knew better; his only expected meeting was with the bottle. The first slug dulled the doubt and in swift sequence he got stoned; got away from the terror inside, and from everything outside by chartering a plane and flying far away to sober up.

The special case history of each alcoholic differs with each personality. But the general conduct of each victim—the nature of the descent and the full plunge into the chemical grip of the addiction—reveals a common denominator of rasping familiarity. Intellectually, the rationale for this drinking is for relaxation, taste or social acquiescence. Under control, the pastime requires no explanation. Once a drinker loses control, he almost never admits it. The grip of control—the pride of the drinker—has been broken. The pacifier in the bottle, passive and available at the whim of the drinker, has turned pernicious master. And the humiliation the drinker suffers at his prostration before it can only be counteracted by delusion, lies and a refusal to accept the truth. It is a fair comment to say that no alcoholic has ever truly controlled the habit until he has learned to admit to himself that he was helpless before its power.

Here then lies the source of the cure problem. At this round in Hamblen's bout with liquor, he knew terror. The easy prideful bravado, the cowboy with the hollow leg, the outdoorsman with the brawn of any two citified bar companions, was being ground into the dust of failure. The illusion crumbled, yet the bluster remained, the tarnished pride still rendered him incapable of admitting defeat. So he ran far away, nourished his anguish and nobody dared to talk too deeply to him about it. But inwardly Hamblen shook with a resentment born and fed of fear.

As to the basic reason for the failure, Hamblen then or now never experimented with the psychological subtleties necessary to find out. Certain evidences—basically circumstantial—do, however, lend a clue. The family environment offered excesses of extremes—the indulgent mother who spoiled him, the stern father who denounced him. The thunder sounds of the full gospel commandments preached by his father must have excited his awe and trembling even as they repelled him. He "knew" it was evil to think the "devilish" thoughts; his father and the Bible said so. And neither suffered for a moment the failing of doubt as to their omniscience. But the youngster was headstrong; he was also bucolic and glandular. He loved living and if what he felt was wrong, then he would simply have to face the eventual fires. The voluptuous delights of these current feelings simply defied repression.

If such conflict existed within the young cowboy's mind, in any formal pattern—especially in terms of his drinking—he remembers little of it. The gamesmanship of his growth and development was not reflection but action—the kind of action that anesthetizes conscience, guilt and such drabness, and gives in return fun, prosperity and indulgence in this world. To Hamblen it was "one helluva world"; it did good for him. It wasn't too difficult to hold off that daily Armageddon between the opposing warriors of good and evil. The most felicitous device had occurred by the accident of design: since his teens he was seldom around his parents and so he was spared his father's censorship and his mother's tears. And, if the inner turmoil boiled hard, there was the comfort of the easy quick-shot pacifier at the bar. With increasing crescendo Hamblen availed himself of it, until it turned on him with fury.

He turned back on it with counter-fury and kept losing. The drunkenness, the brawlings, the scandal-page news stories kept increasing. His shows suffered with his own anguish; the absences, the thick-tongued performances stretched the tolerance of his sponsors. One day he finished a program doubled up with pain. In characteristic style he tried alternately ignoring the "bellyache" and soothing it with copious drafts of liquor. Finally he collapsed. They dragged him off to the hospital more dead than alive, his body poisoned with peritonitis from a ruptured appendix.

There he lingered and, as the months wore on, his money gave out. By the time he was well enough to be discharged, his radio contract was canceled and he was cold broke. He even had to sell his Cadillac—his last worldly possession—to pay his final hospital bill.

"Walked away from the place with twenty-five cents in my pocket," he recalls. "Of course, to say I *walked* away is a slight exaggeration. Staggered would have been more like it. . . . I was that weak. Didn't have a place to go to or anyone to turn to."

He dragged himself through the streets of Los Angeles looking for a place to live. When he thought he couldn't take another step, he saw a sign reading, "The Edgemont Apartments." He managed to make it inside, thinking in his feverish state that he might convince the landlord, or the agent, to put him up for a while on the cuff. He got as far as the lobby and collapsed.

"I guess that was about the smartest thing I ever did," Stuart Hamblen says. "When I came to, I was all taken care of. It was a lady who owned the Edgemont, a Mrs. Nichols—an angel if ever there was one. She not only let me have an apartment on the cuff, she fed me, took care of me, even gave me twenty-five cents a day to ride downtown to find work. The woman was like a mother to me. Much later, when I got on my feet again and the money started coming in, I bought her a brand-new Cadillac convertible."

By the time the mid-forties came around, Hamblen had climbed to the top again. The effort took work and some control of his drinking habits. But he soon learned that his audiences were waiting for him. Serious public figures such as congressmen and bankers don't easily withstand public scrutiny into the seaminess of their private lives. But show-business people, in this regard, are a breed apart. Witness the sagas of Ingrid Bergman, Frank Sinatra, Robert Mitchum, Billy Daniels and Elizabeth Taylor among others; their popularity rises with the peccadilloes of their social conduct. Not unlike Sinatra or Arthur Godfrey, with whose personalities the public identifies—naughty but basically good guys whose hands have been caught in the family cookie jar—Hamblen was seen by his audience as the mildly wicked

nonconformist who meant no one harm ever and in his performances—personal or professional—always entertained.

His new programs, the "Covered Wagon Jamboree" and
"Stuart Hamblen's Lucky Starrs," the latter sponsored by his
staunchest ally, Sam Hoffman, proprietor of the Starr Clothing
Stores, brought him bigger popularity than ever before. He also
was racing his horses, writing songs, living high and handsome in
his accustomed fashion. But this time he took up causes and
blended them into his entertainment schedule. Once he tore into
a group of Los Angeles abattoir operators who were shipping
wild horses into Southern California and having them slaugh-
tered for dog food. For this he was attacked and beaten half senseless by a pair of professional hoods who worked him over with
brass knuckles. Another of his pet targets was the hospitals. Years
after his bankrupting experience with the ruptured appendix, he
remembered them with bitterness and felt impelled to take a slap
at them. Regularly, he would lift his booming voice against
"those miserable institutions that made you sign your life away
before they'd consent to save it."

The emboldened entertainer kept right on striking out, and
with impunity, against any institution that offended him. During
the war, when the fear of a Japanese attack on the West Coast
gripped the area, blackout rules were imposed. One night Hamblen looked out from his hilltop house and saw strings of light
shining brightly down the road and into the valley. He called the
police indignantly and repeatedly and when they failed to respond, he hitched a telephoto lens to his rifle and shot them out,
hardly wasting a round.

Throughout and immediately after the war, Hamblen's stature kept growing, his horses kept winning and he was waltzing
on the old trail that had brought him near to destruction ten years
earlier. Occasionally, in an impulse of nostalgia or a vague feeling of responsibility to his origins, he would accompany his wife
and children to the Presbyterian church where they worshiped
regularly. He had almost begun to tolerate the solemn services
and the "hymns with all those Amens that I didn't understand,"

when a purse-lipped lady walked up to him and asked how much money he was making on his horses. His answer elicited from the pious parishioner a sniff and a disapproving observation that he was tainted by "the devil's currency." Hamblen took off in rage from the church environs and, despite his wife's entreaties, refused to return.

In 1948, Billy Graham, then an unheard-of evangelist, took on the West Coast Babel in his first large crusade. The local papers began sending reporters to the leaky tent in the far reaches of the town to report on the surprising numbers who came forward to be saved at the urgings of the slender, intense young man. Los Angeles seemed hardly the place for such passionate pulpiteering, replete with sawdust floor, massive chairs and Billy Sunday atmosphere. To Hamblen this was familiar territory, the revivalist trail of his childhood; though he had long shunned the fire-eating ambience of such an atmosphere, the swift and easy identification of sin and perforce, his culpability. The preachers, in some irritatingly vague manner, returned him to his father's religious ferocity. They made him aware that he was paddling in the Black Waters of Sin and Hamblen simply refused to engage in spiritual dialogue with them. So he took shelter and stayed away.

But what he heard about this new young fellow he liked. Billy Graham dressed well, spoke clearly, didn't pick specific bad people as his target and emphasized forgiveness and God's love rather than his rage. From his sawdust-trail days Hamblen remembered the stern ladies in the pews with their plain, pale faces, their pulled-back bunned hairdos and their drab Methodist-cotton dresses. The Graham entourage formed a new tableau. The men were attractive—even sartorially elegant—their wives smartly turned out, comely and smiling. They seemed to enjoy living their religion.

"I liked Graham right away," says Hamblen. "Always been a good judge of character and he struck me right off as a sincere guy. Besides, he didn't beat me over the head with the Bible. He knew what I was, what I did and how I lived. He never condemned me. When my horses won, he'd ask me by how many lengths. And when I'd tell him, he'd smile and say, 'That's good.' I liked him for that.

"So I began plugging his crusade on my radio show. He didn't ask for it. I did it on my own."

One night, after Hamblen's show, his wife, Susie, said, "It seems to me you're giving Mr. Graham an awful lot of free publicity."

"Why not? I like the guy. Anything wrong with that?"

"No, except it seems a little hypocritical to me. If you like the man that much, you might do him the courtesy of attending one of his meetings."

Hamblen laughed. "Look, honey, you know I come from preachin' stock. Once you heard my daddy, you heard them all."

His wife persisted. "Aside from that, the fact remains that you tell your listeners to attend the Billy Graham meetings. I'm sure many of them do. But I'm sure that they look for you, and they must think it rather strange not to see you. It amounts to you telling them to do what you say, not to do what you do."

He thought about it for a moment. "OK, suppose we take in the show tomorrow night?"

His wife was right. Many of his fans were there and greeted him. For a while he was relaxed and happy. Then Graham, ending his message, pointed a long, bony finger and warned that only by repentance could the sinner find everlasting peace. It is familiar language on the revival trail. The "sinner" is the unsaved, the unchurched. The description is general and it applies to the mass rather than the few. Despite his own awareness of the evangelistic style, Hamblen writhed—and that night slept fitfully. He secretly returned the next night, and this time sat far back on the other side of the tent, where he couldn't be singled out. Again that finger seemed to point directly at him. Again the preacher warned against delaying the decision.

This time it was almost more than he could bear. For a wrathful moment he felt like storming the platform and shutting this man up. He rose and quickly strode into the cool desert air.

But the irritation persisted. He kept seeing the long finger and hearing the warning words. He took the weekend off and left town, intending to relax with a mountaintop bear-hunting excursion. He did no hunting, but walked in the hills, then sat in the cabin, alone and miserable. Early in the evening he became feverish and sick. "Got under conviction right then," he says. At three that morning he went looking for Billy Graham. He found the evangelist in a cheap hotel in a drab section of town.

"What are you doing to me?" he roared at the preacher, whom he had roused from bed. "I haven't been able to sleep or eat. I've been sick."

"We've been praying for you," Graham answered.

Hamblen trembled as he listened to Graham explain the meaning of salvation. The words were the words of his father but now they sounded real and he felt that he understood them. "You're the only one who can do anything for yourself, Stuart. You can't send a messenger to Christ. You have to go to Him yourself." When Hamblen asked Graham to pray with him, the young preacher answered simply, "I don't think you are ready."

"I could have belted him, I was so mad," Hamblen recalls.

After a few moments of silence he said, falling to his knees, "I'm ready, Billy. Please pray with me."

Graham searched the determined face of the man, then knelt beside him. Together they prayed.

"It was like a rain of lamb's wool falling around me," Stuart Hamblen says. "I was like a shivering man coming into a warm place out of a blizzard. I felt all warm from a fire I couldn't see—just feel."

To those who equate religious conversion with long preparation and an eventual intellectual ascent to understanding, Hamblen's experience must remain bewildering. But to the full-gospel believers, intellectuality is a nonessential factor. Religion, in this frontier-evangelistic tradition, begins with the heart, expressing itself in a mystical, inner emotional commitment, not unlike the mystery of Communion when the wine and the wafer become the blood and body of Christ. Different people are converted in different ways—some instantaneously, some after long periods of reflection. Most significantly, however, the pattern of the change, the anatomy of the transformation, defies orderly analysis. The effect, however, manifests itself because the convert invariably feels a spiritual compulsion to reveal his testimony and what it did to him. As Hamblen reveals it, this is how he reacted immediately thereafter.

He went home that morning feeling new and changed. He stepped lightly, felt a rising surge of optimism and an inner strength that had returned after long years of nagging doubt. He passed bars, open and inviting, without even a thought of going inside. When he put his hands in his pockets to warm them from the early-morning cold, and found a pack of cigarettes, he threw it away without a qualm for his thirty-year habit.

"The only way I can explain it," he says now, reflectively rubbing his massive jaw, "is that somehow I found myself walking the strait and narrow without the feeling of being fenced in. I knew it was really the road I had always wanted to travel but somehow I always took the wrong fork. In those days I drifted there. This time I made the choice and it felt right. I felt free and really happy."

To those who didn't know him intimately, Hamblen's public life seemed to change very little. He went on with his radio program and it continued to be a success. He joined the church and attended regularly and read a chapter of the Bible daily. It wasn't until he sold his stable of horses that he made news all over again.

"I didn't have to do it," he says. "Today horse racing is a respectable, honest business. And there are a lot of fine, religious men who own and race thoroughbreds. I sold my stable because I didn't want to encourage a poor, working guy to throw his money away on horses when it rightfully should have gone for the family groceries."

The whiskey drinking stopped with the suddenness of a tap being turned off. There were times when he could hardly believe it. To test himself, he would walk into a bar, intently watch the bartender mix the drinks and spill some on the bar. He recalled the recent drunken days when that odor would have drawn him to the stuff and he would inevitably succumb. Now he could look at it as though it were tap water. He knew he would never touch the stuff again.

When he felt sure of himself, he talked intimately to his radio listeners about his conversion. Despite the newly found fervor, he restrainedly promised he would never preach at them. "All I'm going to do is try to live a good Christian life." Finally the "good life" backfired. For one sponsor, a cigarette company, Hamblen would read the regular commercial stiffly, then launch into a passionate explanation of how doctors connected cigarette smoking with cancer. "Heck of a way to sell a product, wasn't it?" he laughs. But it didn't discourage his listeners. The cigarettes sold like mad no matter how he ran them down. "Never could understand it," he says. "Guess it goes to show how downright contrary people can be."

In spite of his success, the sponsors didn't particularly care for the new Stuart Hamblen approach to commerce. He went his unshackled way for a while, but then the blowup came. It involved a beer sponsor; Hamblen refused to sell the product. "I know what drunkenness is," he told the top executives at the radio station, "and I'm not going to be a party to helping my listeners become boozers. I got kids in my audience; you don't think I'm going to make barflies out of them, do you?"

It was a hopeless impasse. Neither Hamblen nor his sponsors would budge. In the end, he was sacked.

His most loyal fan, Susie Hamblen, assured him that there were other stations in Los Angeles and other accounts besides beer, and that he would be back in radio before long.

"I don't know that I want to be back in radio," he answered. "I'm thinking maybe that radio and I have had it. I won't sell beer and I don't want to sell cigarettes. And there's a lot more junk that I just can't sell. I can't lie any more, I guess, and I'm not sorry. Anyway, the songs are making money. We don't need radio. And I can always go back to work for Duke," he said with a grin.

"Duke" was Hamblen's old pal, movie star John Wayne. For many of the great Wayne horse operas, Hamblen served as the star's stunt man, standing in for him on all his dangerous riding and fighting scenes. It was a job he didn't have to do once he became affluent, but he liked the action and he liked Wayne, a faithful sidekick throughout the tippling days. When Wayne heard about the "new" Hamblen he wouldn't believe it.

"Hell, Stu, you've been drinking so long you're practically embalmed. What's the secret?"

"It's no secret what God can do," Hamblen answered. Almost immediately upon saying those words, he knew he had just spoken the first line of a new hymn. "Popped into my head as though God Himself had put it there," he says in wonderment. "Later, some joker told me, 'Those lyrics sure don't match your face!'"

The strains of "It Is no Secret," one of the most popular of all popular hymns, became the theme song of Hamblen's new life. Royalties from it and from scores of other Hamblen standards make it possible for him to live a more reflective life and a comfortable one. He keeps a string of horses in private stables for riding pleasure for himself, his wife, his two daughters and their children. His "spread," a mansion atop the Hollywood Hills, once belonged to Errol Flynn, ironically a departed hell raiser in the old Hamblen tradition. From the broad picture window of the den, which faces the great open valley below, Hamblen points to a hilltop fifty feet away. A low rolling laugh tinged with a knowing deviltry rolls from his throat. "See that hill? It's covered a couple of feet deep with glass. Flynn's pals would get loaded here and pitch the empty booze bottles on that hill. It would take a bulldozer to clear it away." The den, converted to a recording studio, is covered by a one-way-glass mirrored ceiling. Flynn would gather his cronies and their girl friends at his mountain retreat, trick an unsuspecting amorous couple into the den and chortle uproariously at the performing pair who would serve as unwitting performers for the voyeurs looking down at them through the glass ceiling.

"Quite a contrast, huh?" says Hamblen with a grin. "Now all you can see is an old country singer fingering a hymn on the organ or splicing sound tape."

When he is home from the trips to the schools, the religious crusades and the prisons, he occasionally mounts a horse and, with his favorite hound dog at his heels, trots into the hills alone to hunt. A particular hunt, in 1963, brought Hamblen back into the headlines again.

In the nearby community of Thousand Oaks, a black Indian panther had escaped from its circus cage. For days it had eluded its pursuers and, with its ravenous hunger, could certainly be expected to attack the first human in its path.

"The whole area is terrified," his wife told him. "Folks are afraid to leave their houses. I think you ought to go out and get it."

"Me? What's the matter with the cops?"

"You know very well the police couldn't hunt down a rabbit, much less a panther. You know how to hunt and you know how to track. People would be mighty grateful if you got it out of the way."

Stuart Hamblen called his hound dog and, rifle in hands, marched into the woods. He tracked the animal for a full day, finally caught up with it, hiding under an old warehouse, and shot it dead.

"Funny thing about that beast," Stuart Hamblen says. "There was a bounty on his hide. Fifteen hundred dollars, and I got every cent of it. Heck, that's more than anyone got for taking Jesse James."

The isolated incident of the hunt for the black panther emphasized in a small way the big change in Stuart Hamblen's life. He hunted down the beast not for the bounty money and not for the sport of the kill. Actually, these were the aspects of it that pleased him least of all!.

"Some things about a man, even after conversion, don't really change," he explains, "certainly not on the outside. I still have feelings and desires; just have to work on them to keep them in hand. Used to be I would think to myself, 'I can take you,' because I was always competing. Now I ask myself, 'What can I give?' My conversion affected not just me, but every soul around me—even my hound dog. You know, before I converted, that dog of mine didn't know any kind of talk but swearin'. He wouldn't listen to me unless I cussed him out in the bluest kind of language. After I accepted Christ and washed my foul mouth clean, that poor hound wouldn't even lift his head when I talked to him nice and sweet and called him by his rightful name. Had to retrain him all over again. After a while, he caught on. He's a changed dog. Like me."

HENDERSON BELK

Businessman, Lay Leader, Student

TO MOST noninvolved observers, the mass nature of Billy Graham's ministry suggests an impersonal wholesaling of religion. The announced lists of hundreds and thousands of converts marching down distant aisles read like war-casualty figures. And the contemplation of such huge numbers too often carries along with it the hazy image of the "mass mind," a generalized picture of the average man with the concomitant common denominator of "average" talent occupying "average" stations in society.

As with all generalizations, the error is implicitly built in; such short-cut deductions block out a distinction between tree and forest. Yet if one emphasis prevails, above all, in Graham's work, it is his urging that the individual maintain the sovereignty of his own will and make his own individual decision.

Since Graham is not in the business of breaking down his converts in terms of their occupational strata, it is not generally realized to what degree Graham has attracted and influenced the highly successful; among them prominent lawyers, doctors, editors, scientists, show-business people and business leaders.

Henderson Belk, of Charlotte, North Carolina, belongs within this group. The Belk name bespeaks dignity and power in the South, representing a retail merchandising empire with sales exceeding $100 million a year.

The drama of Henderson Belk's conversion remains over-shadowed by its aftermath. From financial failure to success it could never have been. All the things money could buy Belk owned; the things money couldn't buy eluded him. However, it is doubtful that he could have articulated his needs in those days; those who knew him best knew better than he. Belk performed tasks reasonably well but seemingly without inner purpose. Such talents as he possessed were mostly hidden or drably expressed. The total impact of his personality reflected discomfiture and in-security thinly disguised by a rich boy's brand of traditional road-show high jinks—before and after his marriage.

The reborn Belk exudes a vivid witness to the effect of God within man. Today he is a leader in his community and in the South, a lay religious force of broad influence, a vastly more suc-cessful businessman than before, an individual challenged by new ideas and impatient to make them work. What amazes his friends even beyond these evidences of skill is the transformation of the physical man into an erect, energized personality who looks both the world and the person talking with him directly in the eye with warmth and confident good cheer. The new life is Hender-son Belk's private miracle.

Henderson Belk is one of six children born to the founder of the Belk empire. His father, William Henry Belk, was left father-less after Sherman's raiders devastated the South in the last months of the Civil War. During the carpetbagging reconstruc-tion period, the elder Belk had neither time nor means to educate himself. He hired himself out at fourteen as a country-store clerk in Monroe, North Carolina. After twelve years he had acquired enough knowledge and saved enough money to open a store of his own.

Gradually he instituted a pioneer system of merchandising tailor-made for the poverty-stricken, debt-harnessed region. His creed was "no credit, no debts." He sold his wares on a cash-and-carry basis. Prices were rock bottom and plainly marked. This did away with haggling at the counters. Refunds to a dissatisfied cus-tomer were automatic. In a sense Belk was the granddaddy of the current discounters. The ambitious merchant reasoned that if he had ten stores he could reap the benefits of low-cost purchasing power, and undersell his competitors. With his brother, John, he worked out a plan that eliminated much of the risk that accompanies overexpansion. Instead of going into a town cold and setting up on their own, they enlisted the money and the efforts of a local merchant as part owner. The store then became privy to the merchandising know-how of the Belk brothers plus the obvious savings derived from mass purchasing. So, in effect, the Belks were not organizing a system of centrally owned chain stores, but rather a family of stores, each of which retained its individuality —its built-in incentive—while the group provided for common benefits.

The phenomenal success of this unique enterprise can be seen throughout the South in its almost four hundred participating stores.

The elder Belk was fifty years old before he married and fathered a family, five boys and a girl.

"I've got six children," he used to say, "but if I had got married at the usual time folks marry, I guess I'd have had twice that many or more. I always said I wanted the same size family old Jacob in the Bible had—twelve sons and two daughters. I didn't do quite half as well as Jacob but that was only because I was a lot later starting."

William Belk's allusion to Jacob and the Bible was typical of him. As he had grown older and could afford the luxury of time away from business, he became deeply engrossed in religious affairs. The Belks were Southern Presbyterians, a denomination more literal and conservative in outlook than their brother Presbyterians in the North. After John Belk died, William Belk busied himself setting up the John M. Belk Memorial Fund, which was dedicated to the aid and assistance of home-mission churches. About 350 of these were direct beneficiaries of the fund.

The elder Belk's approach to religious philanthropy was not very different from his business approach. He never completely financed a church project. His contribution provided the foundation; then the members of the congregation furnished the super-structure. His philosophy was basic: If you contribute to your church, you'll participate in it.

This philosophy was also reflected in the Belk household and in the rearing of the Belk children. Henderson remembers that he was seven years old when his father put him to work in one of the Belk stores as a check boy and a wrapper. Before he was ten, he was waiting on customers. Henderson's brothers went through similar early training. If they harbored any thoughts or ambitions to be anything but merchants, they were kept too busy to do anything about it. After school and on Saturdays the Belk boys were always where their father and their destiny decreed they should be—in the stores learning the business.

William Belk and his wife were good, solid Christians who were also very busy people. They traveled extensively, both for the company and for the John M. Belk Memorial Fund. This was especially true as the six children grew into their teens and required less parental attention.

The effect on children of a dynastic environment is, at best, trying. As sons of a strong, successful man, the Belk boys probably felt the ego-limiting pressure of growing up in his shadow. Henderson Belk, the fourth son, drifted into maturity. He was a tall, gangling—almost awkward—young man who lived in a world apart. As with all the children, he resided in the great house practically until he married. All the Belks lived by family fiat; they lived at home, attended church together and worked in the business. Their extracurricular moments of pleasure were subject to stern admonition when too many local eyebrows were raised after their excesses of worldly living.

"The Belk boys were considered 'fast,' " a female contemporary remembers. "It wasn't that they were bad or evil. They just drank a bit and indulged a lot—if you know what I mean—and a girl from a straitlaced Charlotte family thought twice before she went out tootin' it up with any of them."

Though Henderson felt free in the twilight world of the bar and grill, he shrank in the environs of conventional daylight society. Articulation simply eluded him. Rarely did he communicate feelings or convictions or look even his closest friends in the eye when he spoke to them. He responded to a proffered hand with a limp offering. His friends apologized for him, explaining that he was basically shy. Those less sympathetic accused him of being crudely antisocial.

Like his brothers, Henderson attended Davidson College, twenty miles outside Charlotte. Davidson is a religious-oriented school, rich in the heritage of the Scotch-Irish Presbyterians of the Carolina Piedmont district who had founded it to promulgate their Christian values. Davidson was one of William Belk's favorite beneficiaries; he had contributed to it at least half a million dollars.

Theoretically, Davidson should have been the ideal school for Henderson, but within a year he had dropped out. Interestingly enough, only one of the Belk boys was graduated from the institution. Henderson explains away his quitting: He wanted to join the armed forces reserve and Davidson had no reserve program. Friends in Charlotte offer an adjunct explanation: The school represented one more extension of his father's paternalism, and leaving it was a symbol of mute rebellion.

In any case, Henderson transferred to the more liberal environs of Duke University, where he joined the Naval Reserve program. After graduating with a degree in business administration, he went directly into the Navy. Three weeks before he was to receive his commission as an ensign, the school authorities discovered grounds for his disqualification. Henderson had been secretly keeping a car on the campus grounds. He knew it was against all rules and regulations, but rules and regulations never bothered him. They did bother the Naval Reserve authorities enough to make them discharge him from the program. So Henderson went into the Navy as an ordinary seaman.

Belk saw action during World War II in the Pacific Theater, first with a destroyer-escort squadron, and later with a Seabee battalion. When the war ended, he was discharged from the Naval base in Charleston, South Carolina. He got out of uniform and immediately went to work in his father's Charleston store. The experience of the war had no discernible effect on his personality. He was still the same shambling, almost retreating person as before. When he finally did come back to Charlotte to live and work there, it seemed that he had never been away. The few slight changes were hardly noteworthy: his drinking had become more enthusiastic and he had developed a taste for fast sports cars. His wry sense of enterprise led the young bachelor into a couple of ventures designed to make business out of his pleasures. The first involved buying an interest in a local pub. His reasoning was rational, he thought. He was already one of its more constant patrons; by owning a piece of it, he would have a double interest in keeping contact with his investment. The idea so intrigued him that he expanded his pub operations by buying into a swinging Miami Beach bistro to which he frequently fled to get away from it all. His partner there was a somewhat inelegant character with mob connections. When Belk asked for money due him and didn't get it, he tentatively decided to make a special trip to Miami to dissolve the partnership and force recovery of his capital. He never made the trip. The newspapers carried the story of his partner's demise. Some of his less tolerant enemies had riddled him with bullets in the doorway of his bistro. That event terminated Belk's flirtation with the bar business.

In June, 1949, Henderson Belk was married, while not a few knowing souls in Charlotte shook their heads. Few believed that the state of matrimony would suit him. In his mid-twenties he had been considered a confirmed rambler. Now, in his late twenties, he seemed no less footloose, yet he was taking the plunge.

His bride was Ann Everett of Charlotte. Although they both came from similar backgrounds of solid family and money, their temperaments seemed classically incompatible. Ann was a dignified debutante accustomed to social standing, and she acted it. She was tall, brunette and pretty, and carried herself with an air of gentle gracefulness.

Unlike Henderson, she was an only child, as delicately bred

as a hothouse flower. Once, years before, when she visited Henderson's sister, Sarah, in the Belk household, she had stared aghast as the Belk brothers turned the Victorian elegance of the Belk mansion into a shambles as they engaged in a violent pillow fight. She was even more amazed when Sarah told her that they roughhoused around the clock. On another visit, Henderson greeted her at the front door of the house in soiled bare feet. His indifference to the amenities and his free-living conduct after hours hardly made him the marriage-manual ideal for the polished Everett heiress. Mitigating and finally canceling out the circumstantial evidence was a single fact—they loved each other.

The Henderson Belks began their married life with more than their share of facilities for a full and happy life. They had love, money, social position and a future that seemed as secure and full as a holiday plum pudding. In August, 1950, their first child was born, a boy, christened Thomas Everett Belk.

Most of their family and friends hoped that Henderson was finally settling down. But the object of their hopes conformed to nobody's ambitions for him. Actually, marriage and fatherhood had changed him little. He continued to carouse with his bachelor-days colleagues and would impulsively swoop off on swinging excursions to Miami or New York.

Ann suffered her unhappiness stoically. She was not inclined to "run home to mother" or cry out her misery to friends. But in a small city like Charlotte, it wasn't difficult to keep track of a man's whereabouts or his pattern of conduct.

In 1952, at the age of eighty-nine, William Henry Belk died. His will turned over ownership of the Belk enterprises to his sons and daughter, who were requested to carry on the Belk tradition, materially and philosophically. An excerpt from the will read:

It is my fervent hope and prayer that after I have gone my sons and daughter . . . will use the properties in their charge and possession so that a just and generous portion of the fruits thereof . . . shall be used for the advancement of Christian causes and the upbuilding of mankind.

His father's death and the added responsibility of administering the Belk enterprises accelerated little Belk's pace of maturation. He worked diligently at a minimal level; he continued his program of relaxation at the same neon-lit pace. He describes it as "my period in the doghouse" with his bewildered wife. When she questioned or complained, he responded in the traditional manner of husbands beset by imagined nagging; he sulked, became less communicative and burrowed deeper "in the doghouse." He never slid completely downward and neither did his marriage. Though the Belks presented the surface manners of a unified family, their friends knew that a gloomy gulf between them kept widening.

About this time a new church, Charlotte's Trinity Presbyterian, was in the process of getting organized. A good friend of the Belks, Jean Dillard, persuaded them to become members. Henderson was hardly enthusiastic but he went through the motions of joining. He attended services erratically and he took little part in any church activity. Despite this lack of enthusiasm, Ann Belk's father—who was a power and a leading figure in Trinity Presbyterian—nominated Henderson to the Board of Deacons. Mr. Everett thought that the responsibility of the deacon's office would do much to settle his son-in-law down, give him a sense of responsibility and perhaps prime the pump of his spiritual interest.

Henderson was more surprised than even his greatest detractors when he was elected to the Board of Deacons. He had had no designs on the office and he accepted it with a pale sense of responsibility. He went to meetings and made a pass at posing as a Christian. But it fooled no one, least of all the tight-lipped matrons who sniffed privately at the high-living likes of Henderson Belk.

Belk sensed their disapproval. Though his attendance at church and board meetings diminished, his personal indulgences did not. His marriage staggered on and the Belk family grew. In 1954 the third of the Belk children was born.

A sympathetic friend of his put it this way: "I never saw a

deacon who was snubbed, ignored and covertly insulted by his fellow parishioners as Henderson was. Actually, the post—although well meant—was a disservice to him. He wasn't ready for the responsibility. The congregation resented him. It seemed as though the stone throwers had never even opened their Bibles."

The sympathetic friend was Jean Dillard. She recognized him when others didn't and did her best to make him feel at home and important at Trinity.

Each succeeding child brought with it his wife's hope that Henderson would find himself and settle down. The more tolerant—and realistic—of their friends concluded that it *would* happen—but in God's own time.

"God's own time" came four years later, in 1958, when Billy Graham arrived in town to conduct his Charlotte crusade. Although the Graham crusade stirred up a religious fervor in Charlotte, Graham's home town, it moved Belk to a pitch of absolute lethargy.

"I can't recall having any feelings about it," he remembers. "Charlotte was always having revivals and crusades. I lived through them before and I'd live through them again. This one was no different as far as I was concerned."

But the Graham crusade became different for Belk because of Jean Dillard. She was a counselor at the crusade, representing Trinity Presbyterian, and it was during the crusade that she couldn't stop thinking about Henderson, perhaps hoping to have him see the effect of the Graham crusade. Despite her hesitation to meddle, she called Ann Belk.

"I'm having some people over to the house tonight, Ann, after the crusade and I'd like you and Henderson to be there."

Ann was flabbergasted. "I'm sure he won't come, Jean. You know Henderson. I don't think wild horses could drag him over there to meet a bunch of evangelists."

"We don't want wild horses to drag him, Ann. You just tell him I called and that I'm inviting you over to the house for the evening. You'll see. He'll come."

But Mrs. Dillard wasn't as confident as she sounded. That

night at the crusade she gathered around her a few trusted friends and members of the Graham team and asked them to pray that Henderson would be at her house that night. Among them was Mrs. George Ivy, whose husband owned J. B. Ivy & Co., Belk's biggest competitor. Mrs. Ivy prayed as long and as hard as the rest of them.

That night, after the crusade, 150 people packed the house. They sat on the chairs, the floors, the staircases, listening to Dan Piatt speak. It was while he was in the middle of a talk about God and Christianity that Henderson and Ann arrived. They walked into the house and stood in a corner because there wasn't a square inch of room to sit.

Henderson was scowlingly resentful. He stood there in an unsteady slouch, suffering from the combination hangover of a liquid lunch and the added fortification since then which he felt was essential to withstand the occasion. He seemed to be hardly listening as Piatt talked on. It wasn't until he heard the words "red sports car" that his ears tuned in on the meeting. Piatt was saying that he would love to own a red sports car but some people wouldn't feel it was fitting for a preacher, especially for a member of the Graham team, to go zooming around town in anything so flashy.

Henderson listened intently to the rest of Piatt's talk; after it was over, he pushed his way through the press of people to introduce himself and shake Piatt's hand.

They talked for hours that night. And the next day they had lunch together. It was over this long lunch that Henderson talked seriously about conversion and listened hard to Piatt's words. Henderson's questions were intelligent, persistent and unemotional.

That night he thought it over. The meeting at Jean Dillard's house, the talk afterward, the luncheon session with Dan Piatt— all of it impressed and warmed him. It was nothing like the cold reception at Trinity Presbyterian. The people at Jean Dillard's seemed to care about him. It burst into his awareness, perhaps for the first time in his life, that love could be contagious. The phrase

"God is love" insinuated itself into his mind with unyielding force. He remembered his father repeating it when he recalled his conversion. Although William Henry Belk had come from a strict Presbyterian tradition and attended church diligently, it wasn't until he was twenty-one years old that he became converted.

"I just didn't think I was good enough to join the church. I felt that a fellow, to be a member of the church, ought to be a mighty good person and I didn't think I was good enough."

One Sunday he had listened to an unusual sermon entitled "God Is Love." The preacher, Reverend Miller, had dwelt upon the excuses people gave for staying out of the church, one of them being that they felt they weren't good enough.

"The truth of the matter is," Reverend Miller had said, *"no one is not good enough to stay out of the church.* If you were perfect you wouldn't need to be in the church. But you aren't perfect."

The words settled a doubt that had nagged William Belk for years. That night he visited Reverend Miller, confessed his sins and became a new Christian.

Henderson recalled his father's experience in terms of his own "not good enough" feeling. It was the essence of the discussions he had engaged in with Dan Piatt and the others the night before. No one was perfect, they said, or ever achieved perfection. But a true Christian had to strive for perfection by traveling on the ordered, divine road. Belk kept rolling back and forth in his mind those ideas and his father's experience. After a long silence he turned to his wife.

"Ann," he said, "I'm going to the Billy Graham crusade tonight—and I'm going forward to declare my witness."

She looked at him, wondering if he was serious.

"Well, what do you think?"

"If it's what you want, Henderson, I'm all for it."

Then he telephoned Jean Dillard and let her be the next to know.

"I was overwhelmed," Mrs. Dillard recalls. "I hadn't slept

that first night, worrying that I had meddled. I certainly didn't want to try pushing my beliefs on someone else. Yet, there was this inexplicable feeling that obsessed me, to reach Henderson Belk. And now that it had worked out all right, I thanked God. And I slept soundly that night."

Henderson's conversion was the talk of Charlotte. Those at the crusade, who watched as he walked forward, prayed. Others, not in attendance, prayed for him too, when they heard the news. Still others prayed as they doubted, pragmatically aware that Henderson Belk was one of Charlotte's most likely candidates for backsliding honors.

"I couldn't blame them," he says. "I had some doubts myself. I think every true Christian has doubts. That's why we never relax. We have to keep striving for the strength and toward the perfection my daddy used to talk about. You never can achieve it in this world. But you must keep striving."

It didn't take Henderson long to test his newfound strength. The day after he had declared his witness, he ran into a cadre of his old drinking comrades. They refused to take seriously the religious stuff they heard and urged him to accompany them on one hellbender of a toot. They accepted his refusal grudgingly and promised to try him again. Eventually they gave up trying; Belk never touched liquor again.

The change in Belk's outward mien astonished his acquaintances. The awkward, detached nonentity emerged from his chrysalis into an erect, articulate, amicable man brimming with confidence and an obvious zest for living. And with no need for the fortification of alcohol.

His absolutism about liquor is more symbolic than hygienic. During his preconversion days Belk felt no injunction to humble himself before any nonsecular power. Toward the body he possessed the attitude of personal possession, as with his impulses. He was his own man and in his own interest he pursued his indulgences. With his conversion he felt a sense of responsibility to a higher being and an ambition to present himself before that being with the purest, most disciplined concordance of mind and body. To give up a deleterious habit was to express a form of discipline and devotion, a bending of the will, a willingness to shut out of his life anything that would hinder the full and free capacity of his mind to function. Belk makes no judgments about the habits of others in such matters and never equates such abstinence with spiritual piety. For him they connect—and for him alone he makes the connection.

He became an avid student of the Bible, reading constantly, making notes, applying all the wisdom of it to his everyday living. His curiosity burgeoned and with it his intellectual acuity. As he kept learning, he kept reinforcing it with more reading in ever wider fields. The more he studied, the deeper grew his sureness of the validity of the Christian message.

The intensity of Belk's transformation is possibly explained by the inner personality of the man, and his hitherto inarticulate ability to express it. Psychologists describe underachievers, especially males, as people who frequently live in frozen awe of strong fathers. Feeling helplessly inadequate to cope with them in ability, authority or stature, they rebel inwardly. They take it out not in the manner of healthy rebellion, standing up to a parent in a reasonable dialogue between father and son, giving as well as getting. Instead, they give up inwardly, block out the avenues of growth and therefore the face-to-face contest between the generations on which they could sharpen intellectual claws. They frequently show nothing; they so suppress innate ability that even they begin to suspect they have none. The threatened contest becomes a "no contest." Since they lose before they start, they remain immature in a *nolo contendere* state of suspended growth, and flagellate into themselves an image of supine prostration.

Belk was this kind of classic late bloomer. And there is reasoned evidence that its origins can be explained in terms of the patriarchy under which he was reared. What he therefore never knew was how much quality he truly possessed. His witness to his immediate environment revealed a gilt-edged cipher. With his conversion, the wraps came off, and whatever he possessed emerged, first tentatively, and then, in sweeping arcs of ascension, the full range of his talents: as a businessman, a community leader, a father and husband, and, most of all, as a vital, integrated personality seasoned with a modest low-key sense of wry humor.

To celebrate a hallmark in their lives, Belk went to great effort to have made for his wife a special gold charm bracelet. The baubles represented the incidents in the years of their lives— warm, bitter, funny and serious. It included a miniature whiskey bottle, a sports car, the zodiac signs of their children, faceless women and a cross which represented his new life. Periodically he has new ones made.

In keeping with his Christian decision, Belk works hard to nurture his commitment. Besides his personal program of Bible study and prayer, he readily responds to church-speaking invitations, telling his own story with a candid freedom from self-consciousness. This springs from evangelical zeal; he began it while still in terror of public speaking. Subsequently he engaged a speech teacher, who came to the house regularly to improve his delivery and his platform manner.

Interestingly enough, his commercial activities, instead of suffering from his newfound preoccupation, seemed to accelerate. Probably to strike out even further from the Belk financial establishment, Henderson began diversifying his business interests with his own funds. He invested in several radio stations, auto agencies, motels, in property and a marina; all of them keep making him richer and busier. He enjoys their success and keeps pushing for more of it. He explains it simply. "It's a challenge to invest and build. And I am trained as a businessman. It's gratifying to know you're doing it well. That's all."

With all this activity, he still found time to enroll at Duke University for a master's degree in business administration. For a while he had been bothered by what he recognized as a deficiency in his skill as the store's personnel director. No matter how hard he tried, he seemed unable to feel empathy with the nonexecutive employees. "The problem was psychological and I guess not hard to explain. I was always the boss or the boss's son. I never could understand, really, how poorer people felt. The least I could do was to try."

In addition to formal study and self-imposed programs of broad reading, he began spending long hours in close proximity to the lowest-salaried employees. It turned into a series of on-the-job training interviews for Belk. After intense observation and reflection, he deduced that, although he could never understand them fully, at least he had got much closer, and the knowledge would help him develop into a more humane and therefore more effective personnel director.

In his own church, too, things changed radically for him. He was no longer the deacon, resented and ignored. Now the parishioners sought him out, and elected him an elder. He also sits on the Billy Graham Evangelical Association Board. As his personal interests broadened, a group of his friends prevailed upon him to run for a seat on the Charlotte School Board. He was elected by a substantial vote, and justified their confidence with his energetic service.

The problem of integration was not confined to the schools of the South. It was a challenge that had to be met and hurdled by the business community as well. And the Belk stores had to face up to it. With his brothers, Henderson's approach to staff integration was one of gradualism. Knowing both the temper and the temperament of the traditional Southerner, they devised a stratagem to test public reaction to Negro sales help. They would hire a few Negro clerks in each department. When a white customer came up to the counter, the clerk was available to wait on her unless the white customer showed signs of irritation or open hostility. In that case, the Negro clerk would reach for a feather duster and proceed to act like a menial.

"If the customer was in a hurry, she didn't worry about the color of the clerk's skin," Belk says. "And if she wasn't in a hurry, and not openly resentful, she soon realized that she could get as much courteous and intelligent service from a colored clerk as she could from a white clerk. There is no sense to prejudice. But there is habit in it, and you simply don't break habits easily."

Though Belk, an entrenched conservative Southerner, is in no danger of jumping atop a sound truck and leading a "We Shall Overcome" songfest, he is also in no danger of falling prey to unfairness. He is a warm friend of Harry Golden and admires the Carolina Israelite's ingenious employment of wit instead of a club to overcome prejudice. Also there is the beacon of his faith. In his pre-Christian days Belk could easily have witnessed typical Southern denigration of Negroes and reacted with typical Southern demeanor—indifferent to the marrow. Now it is not political expedience that moves his conviction, but religious commitment.

"Prejudice just doesn't fit into Christian living," he says. "You can't practice one thing and be the other."

Belk's remarkable transformation through his conversion, oddly enough, created one problem at home for every two it solved. Ann Belk was overcome with joy and relief at first. Now she was to have, after years of longing, a serious, attentive husband for herself and her family. In a whirlwind burst from long nights of aloneness, she now had her husband, all right; but she was forced to share him with an assortment of church leaders, traveling evangelists, committee meetings and prayer sessions. The Belk household was forever rocking with them and now she begged for moments of quiet and "normalcy."

"Sometimes I think I'll go out of my mind," she told a friend. "We never have a minute to ourselves. I don't know how long I can stand it."

"Each of us is an individual, Ann," her friend told her, in a church counseling session. "And marriage is the business of learning to live not only with ourself but with the self of our husband. You know Henderson and what kind of man he is, throwing himself wholeheartedly into anything he believes in. Let him find himself—he's trying to. But you have to find yourself too. You must give each other a chance."

She gave herself and her husband that chance by taking a longer look at her new life, gaining the necessary perspective to help neutralize the irritation. Time worked in both their interests. Today, their elaborate home in the Charlotte suburbs and the home at Catawba Lake are somewhat less suggestive of camp-meeting grounds. And, after the early fervor of his conversion, Belk actually craves quiet moments to read and contemplate. His desire for self-improvement continues unabated. The shy, quiet-spoken surface of the man almost, but not quite, hides the bursting activity of his schedule—from store to radio station to church to civic meeting, and a generous amount of time in nonadvertised philanthropic activities. Most summers he is taking extension courses in college. The desire to learn more drives him harder than does a business deal. And during interim periods he flies to different parts of the world—he has been to the Holy Land frequently—to study the geographical sources and the atmosphere that contributed to the drama of the Christian era.

The faith he has found stimulates him to touch, within the framework of his own talents and capacities, every expression of Christian purpose and outlook.

These urgings have captured his interest in one of the most ambitious religious projects of our time: the translation of the Wycliffe Bible. It is an awe-inspiring job, employing 1,800 specialists who are busily engaged in translating that particular volume into two thousand languages and dialects in hopes of finishing by 2000 A.D. The specialists travel throughout the world, penetrating even the jungle areas of Africa to bring the Word. These specialists use, as their base, a 250-acre tract below Charlotte, which Belk donated to their work.

The project fits as hand in glove into Belk's basic religious philosophy. It was taking shape when he first accepted Billy Graham's suggestion to give his testimony before religious groups and church organizations. It was implemented when he accompanied Graham on his Australian crusade. And the Wycliffe Bible will be the culmination of Henderson Belk's own translation of the word "gospel": glad tidings. The glad tidings of Christianity with its promise of goodness and everlasting life. As long as he lives on this side of paradise, he intends to keep talking about it.